Australia's Greatest Landmarks & LOCATIONS

VIRGINIA GRANT

RANDOM HOUSE AUSTRALIA

A Random House book
Published by Random House Australia Pty Ltd
Level 3, 100 Pacific Highway, North Sydney NSW 2060
www.randomhouse.com.au

First published by Random House Australia in 2014

WARNING: Readers, please be advised that images of Aboriginal people
who might be deceased appear in this book.

Addresses for companies within the Random House Group can be
found at www.randomhouse.com.au/offices

Images of the Sydney Opera House appear with permission – Sydney
Opera House Trust 2014. The name and shape of Sydney Opera House
are trade marks of the Sydney Opera House Trust.

National Library of Australia
Cataloguing-in-Publication Entry

Author: Grant, Virginia
Title: Australia's greatest landmarks and locations
ISBN: 978 0 85798 388 6 (paperback)
Series: Australia's greatest; 3
Target Audience: For ages 12+
Subjects: Historic sites – Australia.
          Natural areas – Australia.
          National parks and reserves – Australia.
          Australia – History.
Dewey Number: 994

Cover image © Flickr/loop_oh (Rupert Ganzer) (CC BY-ND 2.0)
Cover and internal design by Liz Seymour
Printed and bound in China by RR Donnelley

CONTENTS

Introduction

Australia is truly a remarkable country. With a landmass of more than 7.6 million square kilometres, mainland Australia is the world's largest island. It is also the sixth largest nation in area – but the smallest continent. Few other countries on Earth can claim to have such geographic diversity; from expansive deserts to tropical and temperate forests, wetlands and snow-covered mountains, Australia has it all. The country's age and isolation have contributed to the evolution of a wide variety of fauna and flora unique to Australia. The vast mainland coastline features stunning beaches, an intrinsic part of life for more than 80 per cent of the nation's inhabitants who live within 100 kilometres of the coast. Australia also boasts an impressive 19 World Heritage-listed sites, which include natural wonders, such as the Great Barrier Reef, the world's largest coral reef, as well as iconic urban landmarks, such as the Sydney Opera House and the Royal Exhibition Building.

The 'greatness' of a location can be difficult to pinpoint. Generally, we consider a 'great' place to have natural or cultural significance, or both. Few people would dispute the 'greatness' of many of the Australian natural attractions discussed in this book, for example, Uluru, Lake Eyre or the Tasmanian Wilderness. Other locations, such as Old Parliament House or the High Court of Australia, may appear less spectacular yet remain significant to our nation's history and culture. In some cases, the greatness of a place may be recognised by only a small number of people. And sometimes a place can be thought of as 'great' for very personal reasons. We have covered as many locations as possible but, of course, there are numerous important Australian locations and landmarks not included in this book. You probably have your own ideas about the greatest spots in Australia. If you feel we have overlooked a place that you believe is 'great', you may wish to start your own list.

Australia's six states, two mainland territories and external territories offer an abundance of eye-catching, mind-boggling places to discover. This book showcases a selection of these great Australian locations and landmarks. With any luck, together with your family and later in your life, you will have the opportunity to experience many of these places for yourself.

VIRGINIA GRANT

'The sun did not know how beautiful its light was, until it was reflected off this building.'

Louis Kahn, on the Sydney Opera House

NEW SOUTH WALES

Sydney

A WORLD-CLASS CITY

Sydney is the capital of New South Wales and Australia's largest city, with world-class facilities and breathtaking natural beauty. Much of the city's life is focused on the glistening waters of Sydney Harbour. Walks, picnics or dining along the foreshore, a splash at a harbourside beach or a ferry or boat ride are all regular activities for Sydneysiders.

But the attractions of the city go far beyond the harbour. The city extends from the Tasman Sea in the east all the way to the foothills of the Blue Mountains in the west. From north to south, it stretches from the Hawkesbury River to the Woronora Plateau. Covering an area of more than 12,000 square kilometres, Sydney offers beautiful beaches, of which Bondi and Manly are the best known; lush parklands, such as the Royal Botanic Gardens and Centennial Park; iconic buildings and structures, such as the Sydney Opera House and Sydney Harbour Bridge; and many other enticing destinations in between. Sydney's approximately 4.5 million inhabitants are a diverse bunch and their influences are reflected across the city.

Sydney has hosted numerous events that have placed it on an international stage, most notably the 2000 Summer Olympic Games. The city has a packed calendar of cultural

▼ *Sydney Harbour*

and sporting events, including the Sydney Festival, Chinese New Year and the Sydney Mardi Gras festival and pride parade, which draws tourists from across Australia and around the world and is one of the biggest events of its kind. The city's colourful New Year's Eve fireworks display gains worldwide attention.

HISTORY OF THE AREA

The first European to visit the area was Lieutenant James Cook (who later became a captain), of HMB *Endeavour*, landing at Botany Bay in 1770. Eighteen years later the First Fleet, comprising 11 British ships, arrived. Captain Arthur Phillip quickly decided that the Botany Bay area was unsuitable and moved the settlement to Sydney Cove – now known as Circular Quay – and Sydney was established. The anniversary of the founding of the settlement on 26 January 1788 is celebrated to this day as Australia Day. Phillip named the settlement after the British Home Secretary, Thomas Townshend, Lord Sydney.

▲ Drawing of Aborigines cooking and eating beached whales in Newcastle by *Joseph Lycett, c. 1817*

Prior to the arrival of the First Fleet, Aboriginal people had occupied the Sydney area for tens of thousands of years. The early British settlers encountered Aboriginal people all around the coves and bays of Sydney Harbour, then known as Port Jackson, and beyond. A number of clan groups lived in the region; collectively they are referred to as the Eora Nation. The Gadigal (or Cadigal) people inhabited the land along the southern side of the harbour, from South Head to Petersham in the Inner West. Although the landscape has dramatically changed since 1788, many places within the city remain significant to Sydney's traditional owners.

Arthur Phillip, who became the first Governor of New South Wales, was instructed to found a penal colony. Aboard the First Fleet were around 780 convicts, outnumbering the 550 crew, soldiers and family members. With the help of convict labour, the settlement quickly took shape. The colony's fifth Governor, Major-General Lachlan Macquarie, who served from 1810–1821, played a key role in Sydney's transition from a penal colony to a free settlement. Many of the city's prominent public buildings and cultural institutions were constructed at his direction.

▲ *Portrait of Captain Arthur Phillip, 1789*

▲ *The historic Rocks area*

▲ *The Australian Museum of Contemporary Art*

THE CITY TODAY

The main parts of Sydney are Central Sydney, the Eastern Suburbs, the North Shore, Western Sydney and Southern Sydney. The following outline covers just a small selection of the city's highlights.

CENTRAL SYDNEY

Central Sydney contains the fast-paced central business district, with office and apartment buildings in a variety of styles from Victorian to skyscrapers; bustling shopping areas; and notable 19th-century buildings, including the grand Sydney Town Hall, built between 1868 and 1889, and the elegant Queen Victoria Building, built in 1898. Sydney Tower Eye is another of the city's recognisable landmarks, offering panoramic views of the city. Circular Quay is an important junction for bus, rail and ferry transport and a destination in itself with fabulous views of Sydney Harbour, many restaurants, cafes and bars and eye-catching street performers. Customs House, at Circular Quay, is one of the city's finest examples of colonial architecture.

On the west side of Circular Quay is the fascinating historic Rocks area, which was established during the earliest days of the colony. More than 100 heritage sites and buildings are found among the cobbled streets of The Rocks. The Dawes Point Battery, built in 1791, is the oldest surviving European structure and was an important part of the colony's fortification during the late 18th and 19th centuries. Cadman's Cottage, built in 1816, is Sydney's oldest surviving residence. The Rocks is now a major tourist precinct, with numerous cafes, restaurants, pubs, souvenir shops, craft centres and a weekly market. Susannah Place Museum provides a window into the early days of the colony, as do a selection of walking tours. In the old Maritime Services Building is the Museum of Contemporary Art, which houses an exceptional collection of modern art. On Observatory Hill, overlooking The Rocks, is Sydney Observatory, Australia's oldest observatory, built in 1858, an attractive building with sensational views of the city and harbour.

On the east side of Circular Quay sits the magnificent Sydney Opera House and beyond this, the Royal Botanic Gardens, a wonderful place to walk, relax and take in the stunning views. Above the Botanic Gardens is Government

House, an impressive Gothic Revival building, which is the official residence of the state's Governor and the location of around 250 vice-regal functions each year. Close to the Botanic Gardens are a number of other historic buildings and sites, including the Conservatorium of Music, the Art Gallery of New South Wales, which is one of the country's leading cultural institutions, and Mrs Macquarie's Chair – a bench carved out of sandstone for Elizabeth Macquarie, who was the wife of Governor Macquarie.

Also of significance to the history of Sydney are the nearby locations of Hyde Park, one of the oldest recreation areas in the city, which includes the Anzac Memorial, Pool of Remembrance and Archibald Fountain; the Australian Museum, the country's first museum, established in 1827; St Mary's Cathedral; the Hyde Park Barracks; and the Macquarie Street Historic Precinct, which encompasses the Mint, Sydney Hospital, the Parliament of New South Wales, the State Library of New South Wales and many fine examples of 19th-century architecture.

On the western fringe of Sydney's central business district lies Darling Harbour, a leisure precinct with numerous restaurants and bars, the Powerhouse Museum and Australian National Maritime Museum and other attractions, such as the outstanding SEA LIFE Sydney Aquarium, WILD LIFE Sydney, Madame Tussauds Sydney and the Chinese Garden of Friendship. Next to Darling Harbour, to the south of the CBD in the Haymarket area, is the bustling Chinatown, the focus of the city's large Chinese Australian community.

◄ *Old Court, Art Gallery of New South Wales*
Photo: AGNSW

EASTERN SUBURBS

There are many interesting locations within Sydney's densely populated Eastern Suburbs, such as the historic maritime area of Woolloomooloo, now a popular dining and entertainment precinct; the nightlife hub of Kings Cross, which has an intriguing bohemian past; the trendy precinct of Paddington, once a working-class suburb; and the expansive parklands of Centennial Park, to name just a few. The area also has some of the city's most popular beaches, including Bondi, Bronte and Coogee. South Head is one of two headlands forming the entrance to Sydney Harbour. Nearby is Watsons Bay, a favourite recreation spot for Sydneysiders and tourists alike.

NORTH SHORE AND NORTHERN BEACHES

On the north side of the harbour, opposite Circular Quay, is Kirribilli House, which is the Prime Minister's elegant Sydney residence. Adjacent to Kirribilli House, at Milsons Point, is Luna Park, an amusement park which first opened in 1935. The smiling face at the park's gates has long been one of Sydney's iconic features. Taronga Zoo is considered to be a leading zoological institution with an excellent reputation for its conservation programs. It is home to a diverse collection of native and exotic animals – in fact, more than 2600 animals call the zoo home. Located on Bradleys Head, Taronga Zoo provides superb views of the harbour and city. Another highlight of the North Shore is the beachside suburb of Manly, which has two beaches – one oceanside and one harbourside – creating the feeling of a separate holiday destination. Running from Manly to Palm Beach, Sydney's Northern Beaches are a beautiful stretch of coastline offering some great surf beaches and a relaxed lifestyle.

WESTERN SYDNEY

Sydney's Western Suburbs encompass the majority of the metropolitan area. The region is known for its diversity, with approximately one third of the residents having migrated to Australia from many different countries. Parramatta is the geographical centre of the city and Sydney's second major business district. Settled in late 1788 as the colony's farm, it is almost as old as the original settlement of Sydney itself. It has a number of important historical sites, particularly Experiment Farm Cottage, Elizabeth Farm, Hambledon Cottage and Old Government House. Built in 1799, Old Government House is Australia's oldest public building and one of the country's 11 World Heritage-listed Convict Sites.

▲ *Luna Park Sydney*

▲ *Giraffes at Taronga Zoo*

One of the best known places within Western Sydney is Sydney Olympic Park, home of the 2000 Summer Olympic Games. The site now hosts the city's annual Royal Easter Show and many other events.

SOUTHERN SYDNEY

Like the Northern Beaches of Sydney, Sydney's southern suburbs offer a laid-back lifestyle, with excellent surf beaches, spectacular coastline and several of the region's best walking trails. Some noteworthy historical landmarks of this part of the city include Botany Bay and La Perouse, the landing point of French explorer Jean-François de Galaup, Comte de La Pérouse in 1788. Cronulla is a favourite beachside suburb with many cafes, restaurants and bars. Near to Cronulla is the Royal National Park, the world's second oldest national park. With its wonderful coastal scenery, this is an ideal place for picnics, bushwalks, bike riding and camping.

A GATEWAY TO NEW SOUTH WALES

In addition to these many great landmarks and locations, Sydney is the gateway to many superb New South Wales locations, including the Blue Mountains, the Hawkesbury, the Hunter Valley, the Southern Highlands, the Central, North and South coasts and, further afield, Lord Howe Island, a truly stunning UNESCO World Heritage-listed site.

HARBOUR ISLANDS

There are numerous islands within Sydney Harbour. Some of these are open to the public, including Cockatoo Island – the largest of the islands and one of Australia's 11 World Heritage-listed Convict Sites – Shark Island, Clark Island, Goat Island and Fort Denison. A short ride from Circular Quay, Fort Denison is a harbour landmark. The island was used as a penal site in the early days of the settlement and became known as 'Pinchgut' as convicts were kept there in leg irons on meagre rations. In 1857 a fortification for Sydney's defence was built on the island, which remains there today.

▲ *Fort Denison*

Sydney Harbour Bridge

A NATIONAL ICON

The Sydney Harbour Bridge is an icon of both Sydney and Australia, recognisable around the world. The bridge stretches 1149 metres, including the approach span, connecting Sydney's central business district with the North Shore. Its deck is 49 metres wide. The top of the arch is 134 metres above sea level and the four pylons reach 89 metres above sea level. The Sydney Harbour Bridge ranks as the world's sixth longest spanning-arch bridge. It is the world's largest (but not longest) steel-arch bridge.

At its southern end is Millers Point, which lies within the historic Rocks area, and at its northern end is Milsons Point, in the lower part of the North Shore. The main roadway has eight lanes of traffic, two of which were previously tram tracks. There are also railway tracks, a pedestrian footpath and a cyclepath.

▲ *Construction of the Sydney Harbour Bridge*

HISTORY OF THE BRIDGE

Government architect Francis Greenway was reportedly the first person to propose building a bridge across Sydney Harbour in 1815. Various plans were discussed and some drawings were even done, but it was more than a century before Greenway's idea began to take shape.

In 1912 a chief engineer, J.J.C. Bradfield, was appointed to the project. Bradfield's unwavering vision and untiring commitment over the years that followed won him the unofficial title of 'father' of the bridge. Initially, Bradfield envisioned a cantilever design, but after seeing New York's Hell Gate Bridge, he was swayed towards the merits of an arch design. Together with the New South Wales Department of Public Works, Bradfield created a general design for a single-arch bridge based on the Hell Gate Bridge. In 1922 tenders were invited for the bridge's design and construction and the contract was awarded to British firm Dorman Long and Co Ltd of Middlesbrough.

Work on the bridge began on 28 July 1923, but it was almost nine years before it was ready to be opened. The first task was to build the bridge approaches and approach spans. The day the two arches joined, 19 August 1930, was one of huge excitement. In 1932 load testing of the bridge began, which involved placing 96 steam locomotives end to end on the train tracks. After several weeks of testing, it was clear that the bridge was safe. The bridge was complete.

Among the many statistics, the following two are a reflection of the work involved. An incredible 6 million rivets were driven by hand into the steel plates and 272,000 litres of paint were used to coat the bridge. The project kept a large number of people in employment during the tough Depression era, earning the bridge the nickname 'the Iron Lung'.

The bridge was officially opened by the New South Wales Premier, the Honourable John T. Lang, on Saturday 19 March 1932, attracting enormous crowds to the harbour foreshore and great fanfare. But the ceremony was not without much drama. Before Lang had the opportunity to cut the ceremonial ribbon to mark the bridge's opening, Captain Francis de Groot, who was part of the paramilitary New Guard, approached on horseback and sliced the ribbon with a sword. De Groot believed that the bridge should have been opened by a member of the Royal family or the Governor rather than Premier Lang. After de Groot's arrest, the ribbon was tied together and the ceremony continued.

THE BRIDGE TODAY

There are a number of ways one can experience the Sydney Harbour Bridge. Visitors can take a pedestrian pathway across its span, a journey of about 20 minutes. Alternatively, they can walk up 200 stairs to a lookout at the top of the south-east pylon. The Pylon Lookout also houses a series of exhibits on the bridge's history and construction. For thrillseekers, BridgeClimb allows one to go right to the summit.

Each December the Sydney Harbour Bridge is a focal point in the city's New Year's Eve celebrations.

▲ *Sydney Harbour Bridge at dusk*

Sydney Opera House

CENTREPIECE OF THE HARBOUR

Situated at the tip of Bennelong Point, the Sydney Opera House is the centrepiece of Sydney Harbour. It is the most recognisable building in Australia and an international icon of late modernist architecture. The building's sculptural form, which features a series of interlocking shells covered in gleaming white ceramic tiles, is one of rare beauty.

The Sydney Opera House has won worldwide acclaim for its design, engineering and construction and in 2007 it was included on UNESCO's World Heritage List as 'a great architectural work of the 20th century'. Featuring a concert hall and various theatres, it is a major performing arts venue.

▼ *Sydney Opera House*

A BOLD CONCEPT

In 1956 the state government announced an international competition for the design of an opera house. The judges selected Danish architect Jørn Utzon's bold, original concept. Work on the building began in 1958, but it would not be completed until 1973. The shell structure's design and construction proved challenging, and costs soon spiralled and the schedule blew out. Relations between the various parties became so strained that Utzon resigned in 1966 before the project was finished. In addition to Utzon's contribution, engineering firm Ove Arup and Partners, building contractor M.R. Hornibrook and architects Peter Hall, Lionel Todd and David Littlemore all played pivotal roles in the development of the building.

The Sydney Opera House was opened on 20 October 1973 by Her Majesty Queen Elizabeth II. Utzon was not present at the ceremony but was engaged many years later, in 1999, to develop a set of design principles in relation to all future changes to the building. In 2003 Utzon won the Pritzker Prize for Architecture, which is the highest honour in the field of architecture.

▲ *Sydney Opera House during construction*

A MAJOR TOURIST AND ARTS DESTINATION

It is home to some of the country's leading arts companies, including Opera Australia, the Australian Ballet, the Sydney Theatre Company and the Sydney Symphony Orchestra. It has also hosted many top international performers. Each year more than 8 million people visit the site and over 1 million attend performances at the Opera House.

▲ *Inside the Sydney Opera House, c. 1973*

◀ *Australian Opera performance of* Falstaff, *1996*

Bondi Beach

A SYMBOL OF THE AUSSIE LIFESTYLE

Bondi Beach is a magnificent one-kilometre stretch of sand east of Sydney's central business district and is the country's most famous beach. Over the years, Bondi has become an internationally recognised symbol of the beach-going, laid-back Australian lifestyle.

BONDI'S HERITAGE

The beach was a popular picnic ground and amusement resort from the mid 1800s.

Prior to European settlement, Aboriginal people lived on the land around Bondi Beach. Evidence of their occupation is reflected in the rock engravings, middens and other artefacts that have been uncovered over the years.

The Bondi Surf Bathers' Life Saving Club was established in 1907. This marked the introduction of surf lifesaving to Australia – and indeed the world – and the activity has become an essential part of the nation's culture. The club – and surf lifesaving itself – came into the spotlight on Sunday 6 February 1938, when a series of large waves swept hundreds of people into deep water. The surf lifesaving club members rescued hundreds of people that day, which would become known as 'Black Sunday'. Sadly, five people drowned, but it was clear that many more would have perished had the surf lifesavers not been present.

Another local institution is the Bondi Icebergs Club, a winter swimming club, established in 1929.

▲ *Two swimmers at Bondi Beach, c. 1930*

A SUMMER HOTSPOT

On warm summer days Bondi Beach is packed with people from all walks of life: Bondi locals, backpackers and families. The south end of Bondi is mainly used by surfers. The suburb of Bondi Beach has developed into one of the trendiest parts of the city, with many cafes, restaurants, bars, fashion boutiques and a weekend market.

Bondi Beach is host to a number of major events, including the City to Surf fun run, the Festival of the Winds kite festival and Flickerfest, a leading short film festival. Spending Christmas Day at Bondi Beach has become a well-loved tradition for travellers and locals.

A favourite activity for Sydneysiders and tourists alike is the Bondi to Bronte coastal walk, which runs from the southern end of Bondi Beach along the cliffs via the beaches of Tamarama and Bronte, ending at the Waverley Cemetery, which includes the graves of some notable Australians such as Edmund Barton, Australia's first Prime Minister. Each spring, the stretch of coast between Bondi and Tamarama is transformed by a sculpture exhibition of more than 100 works by Australian and international artists called Sculpture by the Sea.

> ‘Surf lifesaving by volunteers as begun in Bondi has saved many lives and is now an integral part of Australia's beaches.’
> **Powerhouse Museum, ‘Australia Innovates’**

▼ *Bondi Beach*

The Blue Mountains

SUPERB MOUNTAIN SCENERY ON SYDNEY'S DOORSTEP

The Blue Mountains, just west of Sydney, is a magnificent area of sandstone tableland, featuring cliffs, valleys and waterfalls, and blanketed with eucalypt forest. It offers superb scenery with some extraordinary natural attractions, such as Wentworth Falls, the Three Sisters and Jenolan Caves. It gets its name from its distinctive bluish colour when viewed from a distance.

Much of the Blue Mountains has been inscribed on UNESCO's World Heritage List. Known as the Greater Blue Mountains Area, it covers 10,300 square kilometres and includes seven national park areas and a conservation reserve. It is among the largest and most intact expanses of protected bushland in the country. The Blue Mountains contains some rare and unique species, such as the Wollemi pine – one of the oldest and rarest plant species on Earth and an important factor in the site's World Heritage listing.

▲ *The Three Sisters*

A ROUTE THROUGH THE MOUNTAINS

Following the European settlement of Sydney, the colony expanded rapidly. Land had been taken right up to the foothills of the Blue Mountains, which until 1813 had proved impassable.

Despite the European settlers' early difficulty in accessing the Blue Mountains, Aboriginal groups, including the Darug and Gundungurra people, had inhabited the region for more than 20,000 years. The area contains many sites of cultural and spiritual significance for these groups, including the Three Sisters, and rock engravings, rock art, stone tools and artefacts have been found across the region.

In May 1813 three settlers – Gregory Blaxland, William Lawson and William Charles Wentworth – set out across the mountains. They happened to choose the main ridge and after 17 days reached Mount York. From here they could see the

▲ *Watercolour of convicts building road over Blue Mountains by Charles Rodius, 1833*

fertile plains of the Western Tablelands – the solution to the colony's need for new grazing land. On their return the three men were highly celebrated and were each given 400 hectares of the land. The following year a road was built through the mountains by a convict gang. Governor Macquarie was the first person to travel on the road in 1815; when he arrived at the western plains he proclaimed the site of Bathurst.

A RETREAT FOR THE WEALTHY

During the 1860s a railway line was built through the Blue Mountains, reaching Bathurst in 1876. Now easily accessible from Sydney, settlements sprung up around the stations within the mountains. At first the area served as an escape for the city's wealthy people. In addition to their great scenic beauty, the mountains offered clean air, which was viewed as a form of treatment for conditions such as tuberculosis. Eventually the Blue Mountains became a viable alternative place to live for the wider population.

A SIGHTSEEING WONDERLAND

Today the mountains remain a popular destination for daytrippers and holidaymakers, offering numerous opportunities for sightseeing, bushwalking, gourmet experiences and tours of gardens and historic estates. Some of the key sights are the Jenolan Caves, an extensive limestone cave system; the astonishing Wentworth Falls, which have a dramatic 300-metre drop; and the Echo Point lookout, which offers breathtaking views of the Jamison Valley, including the intriguing rock formation of the Three Sisters. Scenic World, which includes the Scenic Railway, the world's steepest passenger railway, is another favourite attraction.

▲ *The Zig Zag Railway*

◄ *Pool of Reflections, Jenolan Caves*

Snowy Mountains

PART OF THE AUSTRALIAN ALPS

In south-eastern New South Wales, between the Australian Capital Territory and Victoria, lie the beautiful Snowy Mountains. They are part of the Australian Alps, which in turn are part of the Great Dividing Range. Within the Snowy Mountains is Mount Kosciuszko, the highest peak in mainland Australia, reaching 2228 metres.

BEAUTIFUL ALL YEAR ROUND

The Snowy Mountains resorts include Perisher Blue, Thredbo, Charlotte Pass and Mount Selwyn, which draw thousands of visitors each winter. Many people associate the Snowy Mountains with skiing and snowboarding, but it is a wonderful place for bushwalking and camping during the spring and summer when the wildflowers are in bloom. Mountain biking, rock climbing and abseiling, canoeing, horseriding and fishing are other popular activities during the 'off-season'.

▼ *Kosciuszko National Park*

A STUNNING NATIONAL PARK

Kosciuszko National Park covers an area of 6900 square kilometres, making it the largest national park in the state. It contains some stunning natural features, including glacial lakes, large granite boulders and Mount Kosciuszko itself. The first person to climb the peak was Polish explorer and scientist Sir Paul Edmund de Strezelecki, who surveyed the region in 1830 and 1840. It is named after the Polish national hero Tadeusz Kościuszko. The park is also an area of ecological significance, containing a number of rare and threatened plant and animal species. Kosciuszko National Park has been declared a UNESCO Biosphere Reserve.

▲ *Kosciuszko National Park*

A FEAT OF ENGINEERING

Another landmark of the region is the Snowy River, which was dammed as part of the Snowy Mountains Hydro-Electric Scheme. The scheme, which collects, stores and diverts water for irrigation and hydro-electricity, was the largest of its kind in Australia and a remarkable feat of engineering. It features 16 dams, seven power stations, one pumping station and a network of underground tunnels and aqueducts. Work on the scheme began in 1949 and it was completed 25 years later, in 1974. The project involved 100,000 people from more than 30 countries. The Snowy Mountains Hydro-Electric Scheme is often cited as a symbol of Australia's national identity as a resourceful, multicultural people. Although people had been skiing in the region since the 1860s, the influx of workers to the region via the Snowy Mountains Scheme led to the growth of the ski industry. The Snowy Mountains Scheme itself has become a major tourist destination.

Broken Hill

THE SILVER CITY

Broken Hill is the largest centre in Outback New South Wales. It is located approximately 1160 kilometres west of Sydney, near the border with South Australia, in the Barrier Range. Also known as 'The Silver City', Broken Hill was established during the 1880s following the discovery of large mineral deposits.

A 'BROKEN HILL' AND A MINING BOOM

In 1844 the explorer Charles Sturt made an expedition to the area in search of an inland sea. On this trip he named the Barrier Range, which was an obstacle to his progress. He also made reference in his diary to a 'broken hill', which, almost four decades later, would turn out to be very significant for the area.

▲ *Charles Rasp*

In 1883 Charles Rasp, a boundary rider, pegged out the first mining lease at Mount Gipps, together with two others, David James and James Poole. Rasp was convinced the area held stores of tin; in fact, it proved to hold one of the world's richest deposits of silver, lead and zinc. Right away, a group of leaseholders, including Rasp, James, Poole, Philip Charley (who discovered the silver), George McCulloch, George Urquhart and George Lind, formed the 'Syndicate of Seven', which in 1885 became the Broken Hill Proprietary Company, later simply BHP. A mining boom followed.

Visitors can find out about the area's mining history at the Day Dream Mine and at several museums, such as the Albert Kersten Mining and Minerals Museum or White's Mineral Art and Living Mining Museum. The Line of Lode Miners' Memorial pays tribute to the hundreds of local miners who lost their lives while working in the mines.

About 25 kilometres away is the historic village of Silverton, which was established in the 1880s following the discovery of rich silver deposits. It was all but abandoned with the discovery of silver, lead and zinc in Broken Hill.

▲ *George McCulloch*

A SACRED PLACE

The traditional owners of the country around Broken Hill are the Wiljakali people. They inhabited the area for thousands of years but were severely displaced with the arrival of European settlers.

In the very special Mutawintji area, about 130 kilometres north-east of Broken Hill, exceptional examples of Aboriginal art, especially hand stencils and engravings, can be found among the rocky landscape, as well as the remnants of campsites, stone flakes and grinding stones. In an historic agreement in 1998, Mutawintji National Park was handed back to its traditional owners, for whom the site is of enormous cultural and spiritual significance.

THE LIVING DESERT

One of the main tourist attractions is the Living Desert Reserve, situated nine kilometres outside Broken Hill. The reserve contains an exceptionally beautiful flora and fauna sanctuary. It features a cultural trail, which provides a fascinating insight into the area's Aboriginal culture and heritage. Also within the reserve, at the top of a hill, are 12 sandstone sculptures by artists from around the world. The diverse range of artworks is complemented by the stunning surrounding arid landscape.

AN INSPIRATION FOR ARTISTS

Perhaps surprisingly, Broken Hill has a rich tradition in art. One of the city's most famous residents was the artist Kevin Charles Hart, better known as Pro Hart. He was born in Broken Hill in 1928 and died in 2006. Pro Hart brought humour and a wide variety of techniques to his work. One of these involved, rather dramatically, using a cannon to apply paint to a medium such as a canvas. Many of his paintings and sculptures, as well as an impressive collection of works by other prominent artists, can be seen at the Pro Hart Gallery and Sculpture Park.

▲ *The Living Desert*

▲ *Pro Hart in his Broken Hill studio, c. 1980*

Hart was part of a group of five artists – the others being Jack Absalom, Eric Minchin, John Pickup and Hugh Schultz – who became known as the 'Brushmen of the Bush'. The group rose to prominence for their landscape paintings of the local area, which were exhibited across the world to raise money for various charities. Absalom also has a well-known gallery in Broken Hill.

Broken Hill's art scene continues to thrive today, with numerous excellent galleries dotted throughout the area, more than 30 in total, including the outstanding Broken Hill Regional Art Gallery.

A number of high-profile film productions have been made in and around Broken Hill, including *Mad Max 2* and *The Adventures of Priscilla, Queen of the Desert*.

A GATEWAY TO OUTBACK NEW SOUTH WALES

Broken Hill is a gateway for Outback New South Wales, including the nearby attractions of Sturt National Park, Mutawintji National Park, Menindee Lakes and Kinchega National Park.

WILLANDRA LAKES REGION

Also in the south-west of New South Wales is the Willandra Lakes Region, a World Heritage Area encompassing 2400 square kilometres and most of Mungo National Park. It features the remains of an ancient system of lakes, which take striking forms today. In addition, there is evidence of human occupation for at least 50,000 years – some of the oldest evidence of modern humans, *homo sapiens*, in the world. The site still holds great importance for the Aboriginal people of the area today. Also present are fossils of giant marsupials. It is one of only four Australian World Heritage Sites listed for both natural and cultural attributes.

▲ *Pleistocene human footprints, Willandra Lakes*

Byron Bay

A DIVERSE COMMUNITY

In the far north-east of the state is Byron Bay, which became a mecca in the 1960s and 1970s for surfers and those seeking an alternative lifestyle. But the warm weather, beautiful beaches and surrounding hinterland, diverse, creative community and the relaxed feel of the place have since drawn all kinds of people and it now attracts more than 1 million visitors each year. Byron Bay is located approximately 800 kilometres north of Sydney and 200 kilometres south of Brisbane.

THE HISTORY OF THE AREA

The traditional owners of the land and waters around Byron Bay are the Arakwal people, part of the Bundjalung Nation, who occupied the area for tens of thousands of years prior to the arrival of Europeans. The Arakwal people have maintained a strong connection with their country.

▲ *Byron Bay headland*

In 1770 James Cook named the nearby headland Cape Byron in honour of British explorer John Byron, who circumnavigated the world as captain of HMS *Dolphin*. The headland of Cape Byron is the easternmost point of mainland Australia.

POPULAR ATTRACTIONS

Throughout the year Byron Bay hosts a number of events; Byron Bay Bluesfest, which began as the East Coast Blues and Roots Festival, a leading music festival held at Easter which has been running for 25 years, is the largest of these. Byron Bay is also one of the destinations for 'Schoolies' celebrations in November and December each year.

In the lush hinterland lies the town of Nimbin, which became known as the alternative-culture capital of Australia following the 1973 Aquarius Festival.

The much-loved Australian children's book *Playing Beatie Bow* by Ruth Park explores Sydney's early years. Much of the book is set in the historic Rocks area.

The Sydney Opera House's shells are decorated with more than 1 million ceramic tiles.

Sydney Tower Eye is the tallest freestanding structure in Sydney.

In 1992 the Sydney Harbour Tunnel was opened to ease the heavy traffic on the Sydney Harbour Bridge.

The 'broken hill' from which the city of Broken Hill gets its name no longer exists due to mining excavation.

Byron Bay forms part of an enormous eroded crater of an extinct volcano, the Tweed Volcano, called a caldera. Nearby Mount Warning, or Wollumbin, was the volcano's core.

A. B. 'Banjo' Paterson's poem 'The Man from Snowy River' features the high country of the Snowy Mountains. It is one of Australia's most famous poems.

THE BLUE MOUNTAINS FORM PART OF THE GREAT DIVIDING RANGE, AUSTRALIA'S MOST SUBSTANTIAL MOUNTAIN RANGE, WHICH EXTENDS THE ENTIRE LENGTH OF THE EAST COAST.

A member of the Bondi Surf Bathers' Life Saving Club, Lyster Ormsby, invented the first surf lifesaving reel, which became an important rescue device in the decades that followed.

Kosciuszko National Park is the largest national park in the state.

'I have planned a city that is not like any other in the world [...] I have planned an ideal city – a city that meets my ideal of the city of the future.'

Walter Burley Griffin, on the design of Canberra

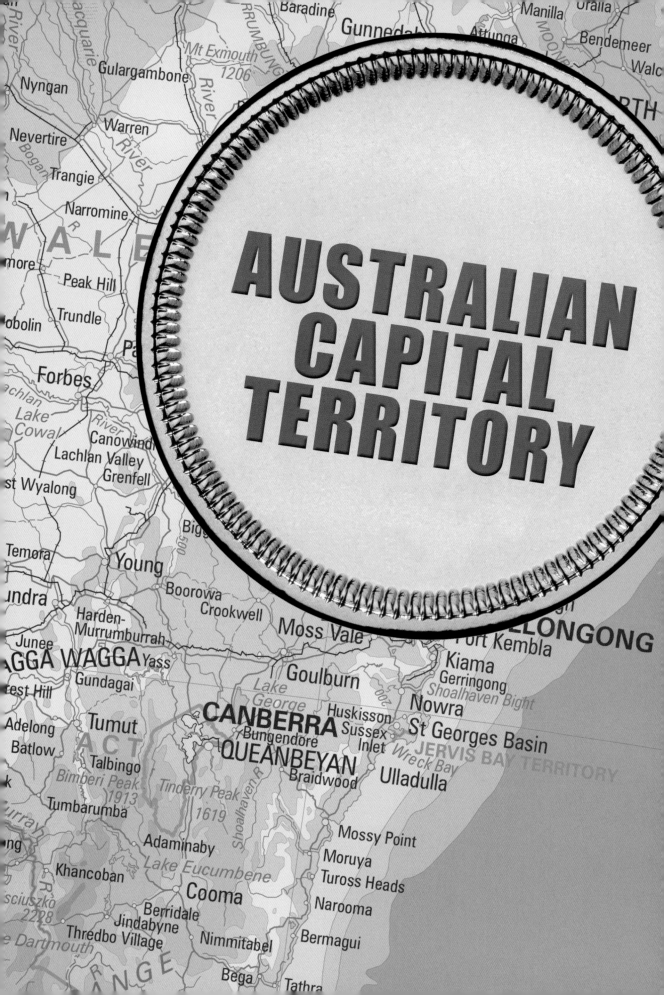

Canberra

A RARE PLANNED URBAN CENTRE

Canberra may be one of Australia's smaller cities but importantly it is our nation's capital. It also stands out among Australian cities as the only entirely planned urban centre – one of just a few in the world.

After Federation in 1901, a dispute arose between those from the nation's two largest and rival cities, Sydney and Melbourne, for the title of the nation's capital. It was eventually agreed there should be a new national capital, located at least 100 miles (160 kilometres) from Sydney, and in 1908 the site of Canberra – some 280 kilometres from Sydney and 660 kilometres from Melbourne – was chosen.

DESIGNING THE CITY

An international competition was launched for the design of the city and 137 submissions were received. The entry from American architect Walter Burley Griffin, together with his wife, Marion Mahony Griffin, also an architect, was selected as the winner. Central to the Griffins' design was the shape of a triangle: at the apex of the triangle was Parliament House, the nation's political centre, and at the sides sat the Defence Headquarters and the municipal, or city, part. Importantly, Canberra's design featured a land axis, aligned with nearby mountain peaks, and a water axis, with the lake as a focal point. It also specified large areas of bush and parklands. Construction began in 1913 under the direction of Walter Burley Griffin but there were setbacks during World War I and the Depression era.

▲ *Walter Burley Griffin*

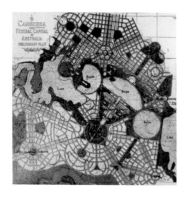

▲ *Griffin's final plan of Canberra*

A THRIVING CITY

Canberra became a thriving city following World War II and today it has a population of approximately 380,000. In the Parliamentary Triangle, Parliament House, the High Court and many other federal government departments and agencies are situated. The city is also home to embassies and high commissions of more than 140 nations. Numerous important Australian cultural institutions – such as the

Australian War Memorial, National Gallery, National Museum and National Library – are also located in Canberra.

A LAKE IN THE HEART OF THE CITY

In the heart of Canberra lies Lake Burley Griffin, a large man-made lake built in 1963 after the Molongo River was dammed. Lake Burley Griffin runs 11 kilometres in length and has a circumference of approximately 35 kilometres. Named after the city's designer, Walter Burley Griffin, the lake is surrounded by numerous important national buildings, such as the High Court of Australia, the National Library and the National Museum. There are six islands within the lake – on Aspen Island is the National Carillion, a striking bell tower that can be heard across the city. Another attraction is the Captain James Cook Memorial. The lake is a favourite destination for picnics, walking, cycling and water sports during the summer.

BLACK MOUNTAIN

Black Mountain sits 812 metres above sea level but only 256 metres above the water level of Lake Burley Griffin. Together with Black Mountain Tower, a telecommunications tower which rises 195 metres above the summit, Black Mountain is a widely recognised feature of the capital's backdrop.

▲ *Black Mountain Tower*

▲ *Mount Ainslie*

CANBERRA NATURE PARK

Canberra Nature Park consists of 33 separate areas of native bushland and grassland. The Nature Park reserves include a number of rare and threatened plant and animal species. Canberra is often referred to as the 'Bush Capital', and most of its residents live within walking distance of one of the reserves, which are popular spots for bushwalking, birdwatching and other recreational activities.

Old Parliament House

A PROVISIONAL BUILDING

From 1927 to 1988 the Federal Parliament was based at the provisional Parliament House, which we now call Old Parliament House. (Until 1927, the Parliament of Australia met in Melbourne.)

John Smith Murdoch, the chief Commonwealth architect, designed the building, which was intended to function as the Federal Parliament for 50 years.

Australian politics developed at a rapid pace and by the 1970s thousands of people were crammed into a space intended only for several hundred. In 1978 then Prime Minister Malcolm Fraser announced plans to create a much larger, permanent home for the Federal Parliament.

AN HISTORIC SITE

The provisional Parliament House was opened on 9 May 1927 – the anniversary of the opening of the first Federal Parliament in Melbourne in 1901 – by Their Royal Highnesses the Duke and Duchess of York, who later became King George VI and Queen Elizabeth (The Queen

▲ *John Smith Murdoch*

▶ *Old Parliament House*

Mother). The Duke opened the doors of the building with a gold key and proclaimed the sittings of the parliament in Canberra open. In 1954 Her Majesty Queen Elizabeth II and His Royal Highness the Duke of Edinburgh visited the city and opened the parliament.

During the 61 years that the building accommodated the Australian Parliament, it was the setting for numerous debates and decisions that defined the nation's future. Several major political events also took place at the provisional Parliament House, including Australia's declaration of war against Japan in 1941 and the dismissal of the Whitlam-led Labor Government in 1975.

Today, the Museum of Australian Democracy, which celebrates our nation's journey of democracy and the history of the building itself, is located at Old Parliament House.

▲ *Queen Elizabeth II and the Duke of Edinburgh standing on the front steps of the provisional Parliament House, 1954*

'It is impossible not to be moved by the significance of today's events as a great landmark in the story of Australia. I say this not only because today sees the opening of a new Parliament House and marks the inauguration of a new capital city, but more because one feels the stirrings of a new birth, [. . .] of a fuller consciousness of your destiny as one of the great self-governing units of the British empire.'

Duke of York, at the official opening of Parliament House, Canberra, 9 May 1927

THE LODGE

Located in the suburb of Deakin, the Lodge is the Prime Minister's official residence in Canberra. Built in 1927 as a temporary residence, the Lodge is a 40-room mansion, designed in a Georgian Revival style by architects Percy A. Oakley and Stanley T. Parkes. It also has more than four acres of landscaped grounds. The Lodge has accommodated numerous Australian Prime Ministers and their families over the years, although not every Prime Minister chooses to live there. It is a private residence but is occasionally open to the public.

Parliament House

SYMBOL OF DEMOCRACY

Parliament House is the meeting place of Federal Parliament and a symbol of Australian democracy. Located at the summit of Capital Hill, the most prominent position in Canberra, the building is the focal point of the city. Parliament House was opened in 1988, the Bicentenary of European settlement in Australia, by Her Majesty Queen Elizabeth II. Once again, a competition for the design of the building was announced and 329 entries were received from countries all over the world. The winning design, in the shape of two boomerangs and set within the hill itself, was from American architectural firm Mitchell/Giurgola and Thorp.

▶ *Parliament House*

Parliament House is one of the country's most iconic buildings. At the top sits an 81-metre-high mast with a Australian flag, 12.8 metres high by 6.4 metres wide.

With 4500 rooms, the building is enormous. It houses a Forecourt, main Foyer, Great Hall, Members' Hall, Main Committee Room, Cabinet Room and the chambers of the House of Representatives and the Senate. The main areas feature works by some of Australia's leading artists and craftspeople. In the Ministerial Wing are the offices of the Prime Minister and other ministers.

Parliament House receives about 1 million visitors per year from Australia and overseas.

The High Court of Australia

HISTORY OF THE COURT

The High Court of Australia, the highest court in the Australian judicial system, was established in 1901. The first sitting took place in the Supreme Court building in Melbourne in 1903. Over the years, the High Court used the facilities of the New South Wales and Victorian state courts. The initial High Court bench consisted of three justices, but by 1946 this number had increased to seven.

A PERMANENT BUILDING

In 1972 a competition for the design of a permanent High Court building, to be located in Canberra, was announced. The architectural practice Edwards Madigan Torzillo and Partners, which was already involved with the design and construction of the National Gallery of Australia, located next to the High Court site, won the competition. The High Court building was completed in April 1980 and was opened by Her Majesty Queen Elizabeth II on 26 May 1980. The first sitting in the nation's capital took place the following month.

Made from concrete and glass, the grand 40-metre-tall building is an example of late modernist architecture. It includes a public hall, three courtrooms, an administrative wing and chambers for the justices.

The main roles of the High Court are to interpret and apply Australian law, to decide cases concerning the Constitution and to hear appeals from other courts, including the Federal Court of Australia and the supreme courts of the states and territories.

▲ *The High Court of Australia*

ARCHITECTURAL SIGNIFICANCE

The High Court–National Gallery of Australia Precinct is listed on the International Union of Architects' World Register of Significant 20th Century Australian Architecture. Other notable public buildings on the list are the Sydney Opera House, Parliament House and Australia Square.

KEY FACT
AUSTRALIA'S
NATIONAL ART
COLLECTION

National Gallery of Australia

MORE THAN 160,000 WORKS OF ART

Located next to the High Court of Australia, the National Gallery of Australia contains the country's national art collection. The gallery houses more than 160,000 works of art. The four main areas that are represented in the collection are Australian art, Aboriginal and Torres Strait Islander art, Asian art and American and European art.

DESIGNING A NATIONAL GALLERY

In 1968 a competition was announced for the design of a national gallery, and a concept by Colin Madigan, a senior partner of Sydney architectural firm Edwards Madigan Torzillo and Partners, won. Although the National Gallery project was begun first, its construction was delayed when the government decided to prioritise the completion of the High Court. The National Gallery was eventually opened by Her Majesty Queen Elizabeth II on 12 October 1982. With the same firm subsequently designing the High Court, the two adjacent buildings make a striking yet harmonious pair.

▼ *National Gallery of Australia*

HIGHLIGHTS OF THE COLLECTION

The gallery's Aboriginal and Torres Strait Islander art collection is the largest of its kind in the world. One of the major Indigenous Australian works within the collection is *The Aboriginal Memorial*, which has 200 painted poles, or log coffins, from Central Arnhem Land. Each pole represents a year of Australia's European settlement from 1788 to 1988, and together they commemorate the Indigenous people who died defending their land during this period.

Highlights of the non-Indigenous Australian collection include works by well-known Australian artists, such as Tom Roberts, Arthur Streeton, Margaret Preston, Grace Cossington Smith, Sidney Nolan, Arthur Boyd and John Olsen. All of the gallery's works, which belong to the people of Australia, are maintained and displayed for the appreciation and education of Australian and international visitors.

▲ *Ramingining artists, The Aboriginal Memorial, 1987—88, installation of 200 hollow log bone coffins, natural earth pigments on wood, height (irregular) 327 cm, National Gallery of Australia, Canberra, purchased with the assistance of funds from National Gallery admission charges and commissioned in 1987*

▲ *Sidney Nolan, Ned Kelly, 1946, enamel paint on composition board, 90.8 x 121.5 cm, National Gallery of Australia, Canberra, gift of Sunday Reed, 1977*

National Portrait Gallery

HISTORY OF THE GALLERY

The National Portrait Gallery contains 2500 works in the collection, with roughly 450 of these on display. The portraits are all of people who have influenced our nation. The gallery, which began in 1998, is one of our newest national cultural institutions, but the idea for a national portrait gallery goes back many years. In the early 1900s famous Australian painter Tom Roberts first argued the need for a national portrait gallery. The collection of portraits was originally displayed in the Parliamentary Library and two adjacent wings of Old Parliament House. However, as the gallery's collection and visitor numbers grew, it became clear that a dedicated, purpose-built space was required.

A NEW NATIONAL PORTRAIT GALLERY

On 4 December 2008, the new National Portrait Gallery, designed by Richard Johnson and Graeme Dix of architectural practice Johnson Pilton Walker, was opened. Located on King Edward Terrace, in Parkes, next to the High Court of Australia, it is the most significant new national institution to be built in the Parliamentary Triangle in 20 years.

A few of the highlights of the collection are portraits of Sir Donald Bradman (1990) by Bill Leak, Cathy Freeman (2000) by David Caird, Ruth Park (1999–2000) by Kilmeny Niland and Her Royal Highness Crown Princess Mary of Denmark (2005) by Jiawei Shen. Among the collection at the National Portrait Gallery, a variety of media, including painting, drawing, sculpture and photography, is represented.

▲ Tom Roberts *by Alice Mills, 1920, National Portrait Gallery, Canberra*

▲ Portrait of HRH Crown Princess Mary of Denmark *by Jiawei Shen, 2005, National Portrait Gallery, Canberra*

National Library of Australia

AUSTRALIA'S MOST IMPORTANT COLLECTION OF DOCUMENTS

The National Library of Australia was formally recognised by the National Library Act of 1960. The reference library had been in operation as the Commonwealth Parliamentary Library from Federation and since its beginnings had amassed a comprehensive collection of documents reflecting Australia's cultural heritage. The National Library Act specified the library's role in ensuring that Australia's important documentary resources, in addition to other important non-Australian materials, are collected, preserved and made accessible.

Today, the library's vast collection contains more than 10 million materials, including books, journals, newspapers, magazines, archives, manuscripts, photographs, pictures, maps, sheet music, oral history recordings and websites.

A LANDMARK BUILDING

The library's present home, located on Parkes Place, in the Parliamentary Triangle, was designed by architectural firm Bunning and Madden. It was opened on 15 August 1968 by then Prime Minister John Gorton. With its distinctive columns, reminiscent of the Parthenon, an ancient temple in Athens, the National Library of Australia is a landmark building in Canberra. Until this point, the library's collection had been stored across Canberra in places as diverse as a morgue and a quarry. Three days after opening, the library welcomed its first readers.

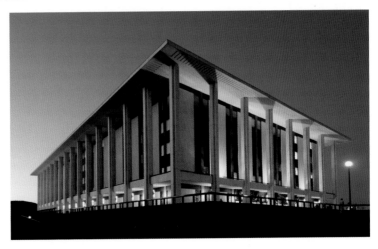

▼ *National Library of Australia*

National Museum of Australia

AUSTRALIA'S MOST IMPORTANT ARTEFACTS

On Canberra's Acton Peninsula, next to the Australian National University, sits the National Museum of Australia. Open since 11 March 2001, and with a total of 6600 square metres of exhibition space, it holds a huge collection of artefacts that reflect Australia's social history. Our Indigenous heritage, the history of European settlement in Australia and influential people and events are all represented. The collections cover themes as diverse as the history of agriculture, industry, science and technology and crime.

▲ *Debrie Parvo model L-35-millimetre camera used by Frank Hurley from 1929*

A STRIKING DESIGN

The National Museum of Australia was designed by architects Ashton Raggatt McDougall and Robert Peck von Hartel Trethowan. The post-modern building's exterior features a dramatic sculptural loop that reaches 30 metres high, inspired by Uluru. In the entrance hall is an enormous rope knot that reflects the idea that there is no single story of Australia's history but many strands bound together. Colour and texture are important elements of the building's design, reflecting the Australian landscape itself.

▼ *National Museum of Australia, Canberra*

Canberra's embassies

EMBASSIES, HIGH COMMISSIONS AND DIPLOMATIC MISSIONS

There are more than 80 embassies, high commissions (in the case of Commonwealth countries) and diplomatic missions in Canberra. Most of them are located in the suburb of Yarralumla. Although many visitors to Canberra enjoy viewing the embassies and high commissions, the primary purpose of the foreign missions is to represent their nation in Australia and to offer advice and assistance to citizens and visitors from their country.

HISTORY OF DIPLOMACY IN CANBERRA

In 1930 Britain appointed its first Canberra-based official representative. Following World War II, the diplomatic presence in Canberra grew quickly. The United States was

▼ *Embassy of the United States, Canberra*

the first country to establish an embassy in the capital. The stately architecture of the Embassy of the United States, an adapted Georgian style, is inspired by colonial 17th- and 18th- century buildings in the south of the United States.

Other countries followed the United States' lead and built their embassies in an architectural style that is typical of their national heritage. Some of the buildings are traditional, such as the Embassy of the People's Republic of China, which draws on ancient Chinese architecture, while others are modern. The High Commission of Papua New Guinea, which is popular with visitors, has been built in the style of a traditional spirit house – a meeting place for elders and a storehouse for sacred objects.

▲ *Aboriginal Tent Embassy, 1996*

▲ *Aboriginal Tent Embassy, 2001*

ABORIGINAL TENT EMBASSY

On 26 January 1972 four Indigenous activists set up a beach umbrella on the lawns in front of the then Parliament House – what we now call Old Parliament House – in protest against the McMahon-led Government's decision to reject a proposal for Indigenous land rights. The protest successfully brought the issue of Indigenous land rights to national awareness and tents were erected as more and more people joined the protest. Over the years the unofficial embassy was relocated to several sites, but in 1992, on the 20th anniversary of its founding, it returned to its original location on the lawn of Old Parliament House. The embassy has been a frequent subject of controversy, with many calling for its removal or replacement with a more permanent structure in another setting.

The Australian War Memorial

KEY FACT
THE NATIONAL
WAR MEMORIAL
AND ARCHIVE

REMEMBERING AUSTRALIANS IN WAR

Located in the Canberra suburb of Campbell, the Australian War Memorial commemorates the sacrifice made by Australians who have participated in war. It aims to help Australians to remember and understand our nation's wartime experiences and their lasting effects on individuals and communities. The memorial, which opened in 1941, includes a commemorative area, museum and research centre.

In the commemorative area is the Hall of Memory, a stunning space – surrounded by a mosaic of more than 6 million tiles and stained-glass windows and topped by a decorated dome – designed to encourage quiet contemplation. At the centre of the Hall of Memory lies the Tomb of the Unknown Australian Soldier – an actual tomb of an unidentified soldier whose remains were moved from a war cemetery in France – in remembrance of the Australians who have lost their lives during war. Surrounding the courtyard is a long series of bronze panels – the Roll of Honour. It lists the names of almost all of the Australian men and women who have been killed during service since 1885, more than 102,000 in total.

▲ *Australian War Memorial*

THE COLLECTION

The memorial's galleries preserve an extensive collection of Australian wartime memorabilia – everything from letters, photographs and diaries right through to entire World War II aircraft. Importantly, the documents and artefacts tell of the courage, achievements, suffering and sacrifices of Australians during conflicts.

IMPORTANT CEREMONIES

Ceremonies are held at the Australian War Memorial on Anzac Day (25 April) and Remembrance Day (11 November) and include the laying of a wreath at the Tomb of the Unknown Australian Soldier.

▲ *Roll of Honour*

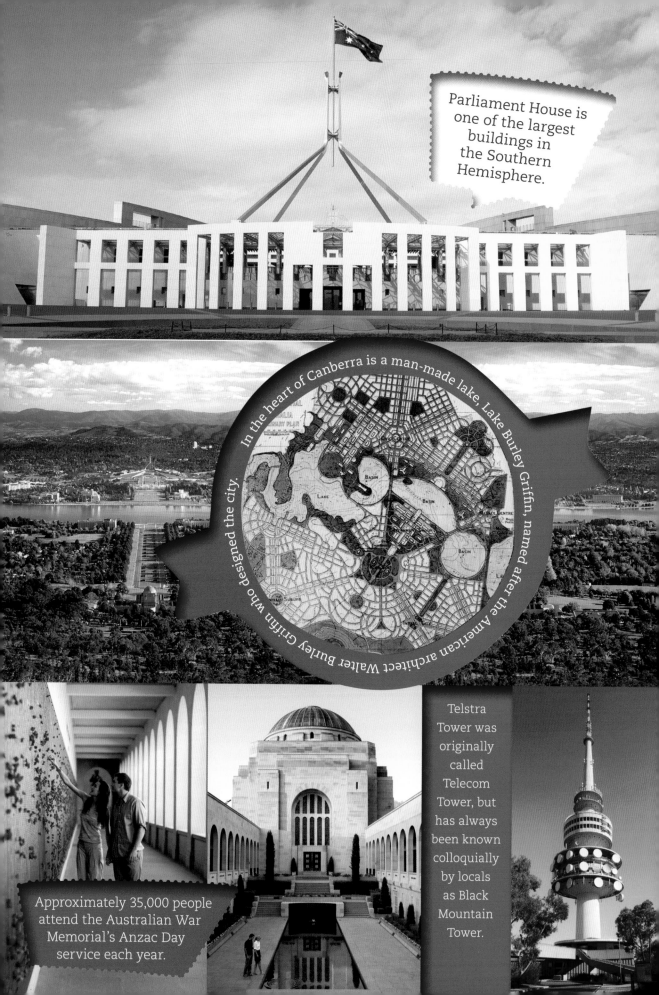

Parliament House is one of the largest buildings in the Southern Hemisphere.

In the heart of Canberra is a man-made lake, Lake Burley Griffin, named after the American architect Walter Burley Griffin who designed the city.

Approximately 35,000 people attend the Australian War Memorial's Anzac Day service each year.

Telstra Tower was originally called Telecom Tower, but has always been known colloquially by locals as Black Mountain Tower.

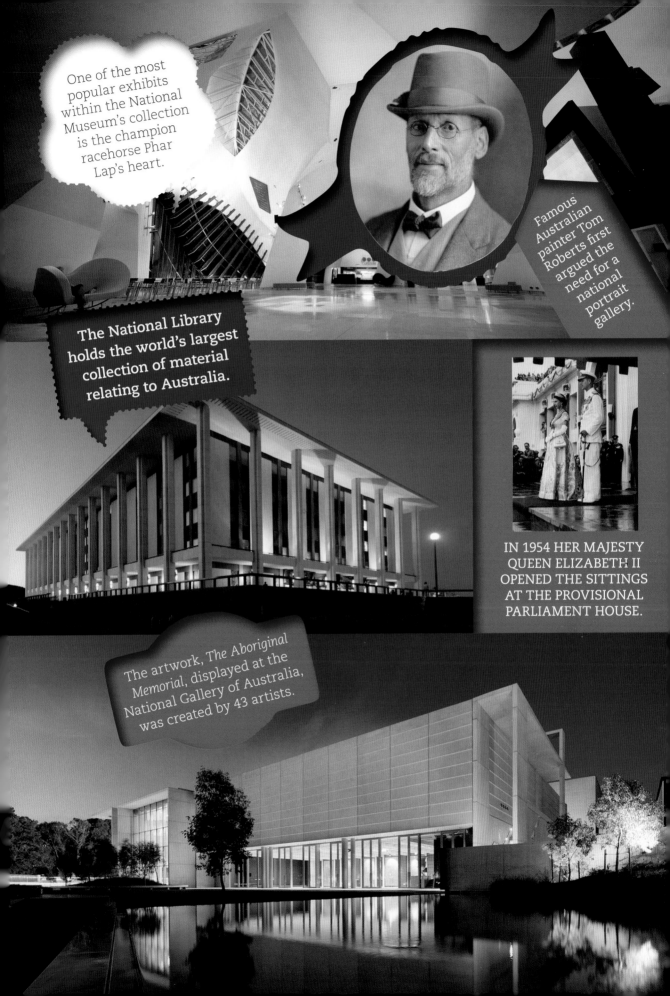

One of the most popular exhibits within the National Museum's collection is the champion racehorse Phar Lap's heart.

Famous Australian painter Tom Roberts first argued the need for a national portrait gallery.

The National Library holds the world's largest collection of material relating to Australia.

IN 1954 HER MAJESTY QUEEN ELIZABETH II OPENED THE SITTINGS AT THE PROVISIONAL PARLIAMENT HOUSE.

The artwork, *The Aboriginal Memorial*, displayed at the National Gallery of Australia, was created by 43 artists.

'From a high forest-hill, about a mile east of our route, I first obtained a complete view of a noble range of mountains, rising in the south to a stupendous height, and presenting as bold and picturesque an outline as ever [a] painter imagined.'

Sir Thomas Mitchell, on the Grampians

VICTORIA

Melbourne

'MARVELLOUS MELBOURNE'

Melbourne is the capital of Victoria and Australia's second largest city, perhaps known best for its fascinating streets, extensive tram network, well-preserved heritage buildings and contemporary architecture, magnificent public gardens and of course the Yarra River. Melbourne is often described as being a city of 'hidden gems'. Indeed, much life – cafes, restaurants, bars and boutiques – can be discovered among the city's laneways and historic arcades. The city has a thriving cultural scene which is evident in its many leading museums and galleries right through to the renowned street art.

Today more than 4 million people call Melbourne home, with many different nationalities represented. In recent years Melbourne has ranked in top position in the Economist Intelligence Unit's index of the world's most liveable cities (City Liveability Index). In general, Melburnians, as the city's residents are known, love their food, shopping and sport. Melbourne has some of Australia's best restaurants and a strong cafe culture, which became entrenched following the influx of post-war European immigrants. The city's cultural

▼ *Melbourne skyline*

diversity is reflected in the array of food outlets – Chinese, Vietnamese, Italian and Greek are just a few of the choices on offer. With a reputation for cutting-edge fashion, the city attracts visitors from all over the country with a specific mission in mind: shopping. The main shopping district lies within Collins, Bourke, Swanston and Elizabeth streets, but other noteworthy shopping areas include the boutiques of Chapel Street, South Yarra and the factory outlets of Bridge Road, Richmond. Another favourite Melbourne shopping haunt for locals and tourists is the historic Queen Victoria Market, opened in 1878. Finally, Melbourne hosts some of the most important events on the sporting calendar, such as the Australian Open, the Australian Grand Prix, the AFL Grand Final, the Melbourne Cup and the Boxing Day Test.

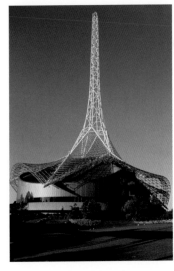

▲ *The Arts Centre Melbourne*

TRADITIONAL OWNERS

Prior to European settlement, the area around Port Phillip Bay was occupied by a number of Aboriginal groups, including the Wurundjeri, the Boonerwrung, Taungurong, Djajawurrung and Wathaurong people, together comprising the Kulin Nation, for tens of thousands of years. The area provided a rich source of food and water and served as a meeting place. Although the land appears vastly different today, evidence of the traditional owners remains – the shell middens around Port Phillip Bay and the scarred trees, such as in Fitzroy Gardens, are two such examples. One can learn more about the city's original inhabitants at the Koorie Heritage Trust Cultural Centre and the Bunjilaka Aboriginal Cultural Centre at the fabulous Melbourne Museum.

▲ *Engraving of John Batman's treaty with the local Aboriginal people, 1835*

THE HISTORY OF MELBOURNE

An attempt was made by Lieutenant David Collins to settle within Port Phillip Bay in 1803. However, the site proved to be difficult for the party of soldiers, convicts and free settlers and the following year the settlement was abandoned for one on the Derwent River in Van Diemen's Land (as Tasmania was originally known) – which would ultimately become Hobart.

In 1835 a group of settlers, led by John Batman, arranged the 'purchase' of land from local Aboriginal people and a settlement was established on the banks of the Yarra River. Although the settlement was unsanctioned by the authorities, by 1837 there was little choice but to accept it. An official survey of the area was undertaken and Governor Bourke declared the township as the capital of the Port Phillip District of New South Wales, naming it after the British Prime Minister William Lamb, the second Viscount Melbourne. In 1847 Melbourne was proclaimed a city by Queen Victoria. In 1851 the Colony of Victoria was declared and Melbourne was announced as its capital. The Aboriginal people who occupied the region were swiftly forced off their traditional land and, in what was a very sad chapter of Australia's history, many were rounded up and imprisoned or killed.

THE BOOM YEARS

▲ *Flinders Street Station*

Following the discovery of gold in Victoria during the 1850s, Melbourne experienced unprecedented growth. There was a steady stream of arrivals into the port, mostly from Britain, who dreamed of striking it rich. The city became a bustling metropolis, transformed by the appearance of stately buildings and lavish decoration, particularly along Collins and Bourke streets – symbols of the colony's newfound wealth. Important infrastructure was also created, including gas street lighting and piped water, to service the rapidly growing city. Quite suddenly, the city took its place on the international stage as 'Marvellous Melbourne', one of the richest cities in the world. By 1890 Melbourne's population was approaching half a million people and it was the second largest city in the British Empire.

The gold rush boom ground to a halt in the 1890s, but Melbourne continued to prosper over the years. After Federation, from 1901 until 1927, the city was the seat of government for Australia. Following World War II, Melbourne attracted significant numbers of migrants, mostly from Italy and Greece, who have contributed to the city's cultural diversity.

MELBOURNE TODAY

Melbourne's central business district is situated on the north bank of the Yarra River. Flinders Street Station, on the corner of Flinders and Swanston streets, is the hub of Melbourne's suburban rail network and a landmark of the city. The elegant building dates from 1910, but even before then the site was used as Australia's first steam rail station. Across from Flinders Street Station stand three other Melbourne landmarks: the historic Young and Jacksons Hotel, the Gothic St Paul's Cathedral and, the newest arrival, Federation Square, known to locals as 'Fed Square'. Federation Square is a large public space surrounded by cafes, restaurants, bars, retail outlets and the Ian Potter Centre: NGV (National Gallery of Victoria) Australia and the Australian Centre for the Moving Image. A diverse range of events has been held at the space since its opening in 2002. It is now the city's top attraction for national and international visitors.

On the southern bank of the Yarra River, opposite Flinders Street Station, is Southbank, a more recently developed part of the city. A leisure precinct, Southbank has many cafes, restaurants, shops, a number of prominent cultural institutions and the sparkling Crown Casino. Some of the main cultural venues within the vicinity are the Arts Centre Melbourne, the Melbourne Recital Centre, the National Gallery of Victoria, the CUB Malthouse, the Australian Centre for Contemporary Art and the Victorian College of the Arts. High-rise buildings have popped up right across Southbank; unmissable is Eureka Tower, a 297-metre-high tower. At the top of the tower a platform affords panoramic views of the city and its surrounds.

Docklands – previously the historic Victoria Dock, which had become dilapidated – is part of a major urban renewal project to extend the CBD along the waterfront. Several new landmarks have emerged from the development, including Docklands Stadium, presently Etihad Stadium, and Southern Cross Station.

▲ *Webb Bridge, Docklands*

◀ *Federation Square*

HERITAGE ARCHITECTURE

There are many excellent examples of heritage architecture throughout the city. Built in 1862, the Old Treasury Building, on Spring Street, is considered to be one of the finest public buildings in Australia. Also on Spring Street, the Parliament of Victoria, which was constructed between 1856 and 1929 but never fully completed, is another important historical building

▲ Old Melbourne Gaol

– home to the Australian Parliament until the opening of Parliament House in Canberra in 1927. Old Melbourne Gaol is one of the city's oldest surviving buildings. Now a museum, the bluestone building served as a prison from 1842 to 1929, during which time it held the likes of notorious bushranger Ned Kelly, who was hanged at the site. The Royal Exhibition Building in Carlton Gardens is yet another highly significant historical building, detailed in the following pages.

OTHER MELBOURNE HIGHLIGHTS

Beyond Melbourne's CBD, highlights include Lygon Street, Carlton, a bustling precinct famous for its Italian restaurants; the creative hub of Fitzroy; the leafy, exclusive pockets of South Yarra and Toorak; and the vibrant suburb of St Kilda, home to the historic St Kilda Sea Baths and the iconic amusement park, Luna Park.

THE MCG

Built in 1852, the Melbourne Cricket Ground, also known as the MCG or simply the 'G, is a national icon. At least twice each year the nation's focus is on the stadium: in September when it hosts the Australian Football League

▲ Melbourne Cricket Ground

(AFL) grand final, and again in December, for the Boxing Day Test. Although the ground is synonymous with AFL and cricket, over the years it has hosted many other significant sporting events, notably the 1956 Melbourne Summer Olympic Games and 2006 Commonwealth Games. Additionally, some of the world's greatest artists have performed at the MCG. The ground is much loved by the city's sports-mad residents.

Royal Exhibition Building and Carlton Gardens

ROYAL EXHIBITION BUILDING

North of Melbourne's central business district, in Carlton Gardens, is the magnificent Royal Exhibition Building, one of the oldest surviving exhibition buildings in the world. In 2004 it was the first building in the country to be inscribed on UNESCO's World Heritage List.

The Royal Exhibition Building stands out as one of the few monuments of the international exhibitions movement of the mid 19th century – sometimes referred to as the golden age of fairs – that remains true to its original condition and within its original context. It was built for the Melbourne International Exhibition of 1880. Intended to showcase Melbourne as a sophisticated, progressive city, the event was modelled on the Great Exhibition of 1851, also known as the Crystal Palace Exhibition, in Hyde Park, London. In 1888 the Royal Exhibition Building hosted the Melbourne Centennial International Exhibition. At the time of its construction it was the tallest building in the city.

▲ *Royal Exhibition Building*

The building's elaborate design, by architect Joseph Reed, was influenced by a number of styles, including the German *Rundbogenstil* and Italian Renaissance. It has a great hall and four grand entrance porticoes. It also has an enormous dome, based on the Florence Cathedral dome. Reed also designed the Melbourne Town Hall and State Library of Victoria.

Over the years the building has hosted many diverse public events, including state receptions, balls, concerts, art exhibitions and trade shows. It was chosen for the opening of the first Commonwealth Parliament of Australia, on 9 May 1901, an historic event which attracted enormous public interest, with 12,000 people in attendance. It was also used to accommodate patients during the Spanish influenza pandemic of 1919 and as a venue for several sports during the 1956 Olympic Games. The fact it continues to function as a venue for exhibitions and large events is unusual for buildings of its kind.

The Melbourne International Flower and Garden Show – the largest horticultural event in the Southern Hemisphere – is just one of the many events held at the site each year.

CARLTON GARDENS

The Royal Exhibition Building is set within formal gardens, known as Carlton Gardens. The gardens are a superb example of Victorian landscape design. Also designed by architect Joseph Reed, together with William Sangster, they were intended to complement the building, with tree-lined paths, fountains, structured garden beds and two ornamental lakes. They feature a range of European and native species.

Also located in the gardens is the acclaimed Melbourne Museum, which has a gallery dedicated to children's interests.

▼ *Royal Exhibition Building*

The Dandenong Ranges and Yarra Valley

KEY FACT
LEADING
AUSTRALIAN
WINE REGION

ESCAPE FROM THE CITY

The Dandenong Ranges, just east of Melbourne, and the Yarra Valley, to the north-east, are charming locations with beautiful scenery and unique attractions. Both are popular destinations for daytrips and weekend stays.

THE DANDENONG RANGES

The Dandenong Ranges feature picturesque cool-climate gardens and magnificent natural forest. The area is known for its fern gullies and towering mountain ash trees, a species of eucalyptus, which are among the tallest trees in the world. Walks and picnics in the Dandenong Ranges National Park are favourite activities. From Mount Dandenong, which rises to 633 metres, visitors can gain breathtaking views, including back to the city. The mountain usually receives light to moderate snowfall several times a year.

THE YARRA VALLEY

The Yarra Valley produces some of Australia's top cool-climate wines. With more than 40 wineries in the region, cellar door tastings and dining at vineyard restaurants are the main attractions.

Beyond the many cafe and restaurant dining options, the local produce is outstanding, much of which can be enjoyed directly at the farm.

The Yarra Valley offers plenty of attractive scenery, with rolling green pastures, forests and, of course, abundant grapevines. Some visitors choose to experience the landscape from above, taking sunrise hot air balloon flights. The Healesville Sanctuary, set among 30 hectares of bushland, is renowned as a place where visitors can experience Australia's wildlife close up.

▼ *Yarra Valley vines*

Mornington Peninsula

A MUCH-LOVED GETAWAY DESTINATION

Just over an hour's drive from Melbourne is the Mornington Peninsula, a much-loved destination for weekend and holiday getaways for the city's residents. Known to Melburnians simply as 'the peninsula', it has various charming coastal villages and towns, some with a Mediterranean feel; Portsea and Sorrento are two of the best known.

HIGHLIGHTS OF THE PENINSULA

▲ *Mount Martha Beach*

The peninsula boasts a variety of beaches, from the popular, sheltered beaches of Port Phillip Bay to the west, to the wild beaches of Bass Strait to the south and the less frequented beaches of Western Port to the east. Swimming, snorkelling, scuba diving, boating and fishing are all favourite activities during the summer. Arthurs Seat is the highest point on the peninsula, with stunning views from the summit, stretching as far as Melbourne on clear days. In the hinterland, around Red Hill, there are many cool-climate vineyards. Cellar door wine tastings and picking local produce are relaxing activities during the winter months.

A number of national parks are located within the region, with stunning coastal scenery, an array of plants and wildlife and some fascinating historical links. Of particular note is Point Nepean National Park, at the very tip of the Mornington Peninsula. It features a number of heritage buildings, including a quarantine station and military fortifications. The quarantine station served a vital role in protecting the colony from disease carried by the many immigrants arriving via ship during the 19th century. The heavy fortifications at Point Nepean, built in the 1870s, led to reports that Melbourne was the best defended city in the British Empire. It was also within this park area, at Cheviot Beach, that Australia's Prime Minister, Harold Holt, disappeared in the surf on 17 December 1967. His body was never located. A memorial to the former Prime Minister stands at Cheviot Hill.

Phillip Island and Wilsons Promontory

A MAGNIFICENT ECOTOURISM CENTRE

Situated approximately 140 kilometres south-east of Melbourne, Phillip Island is an ecotourism centre. The island is famous for its colony of little penguins, also known as fairy penguins, which is estimated to number 32,000. In addition to penguins, the island supports a range of other native wildlife, including the country's biggest colony of Australian fur seals, with an estimated 10–12,000 of the species at Seal Rocks. A BirdLife International Important Bird Area has been declared along the south coast of the island for its role in providing a habitat for large populations of hooded plovers, short-tailed shearwaters (commonly referred to as mutton-birds), Pacific gulls and little penguins. The scenery is quite magnificent, with windswept coastline, wetlands and woodlands to explore.

▼ *Fur seals on Phillip Island*

Today, Phillip Island Nature Parks offer a variety of animal encounters, such as the daily sunset Penguin Parade – a remarkable procession of the little penguins as they return to their burrows in the sand dunes – the Koala Conservation Centre, Churchill Island Heritage Farm and Nobbies Centre, for seals and other marine life.

HISTORY OF THE ISLAND

The original inhabitants of the island were the Boonerwrung people, who visited during the summer months to hunt for animals, particularly mutton-birds. The first European to explore the area was George Bass in 1798, who named Western Port. Soon after Bass's visit, the sealers moved in, hunting the seals around Seal Rocks for their skin and oil. European settlers arrived in the Western Port area during the 1840s, disrupting the traditional owners' way of life.

MOTOR RACING

The island also has strong ties with motor racing. For a number of years it was home to the Australian Grand Prix. Today, the Phillip Island Grand Prix Circuit hosts a number of motor sport events, including the Australian Motorcycle Grand Prix, the World Superbike Championship, V8 Supercars and the Phillip Island Classic.

WILSONS PROMONTORY

Not far from Phillip Island, on the mainland, is Wilsons Promontory, known to locals as 'the Prom', a remote area of great natural beauty. South Point, the tip of the peninsula, is the southernmost part of mainland Australia. Wilsons Promontory National Park covers most of the peninsula, which features spectacular

▲ *Sand trail in Wilsons Promontory*

coastal scenery, mountains and forest. The land has great significance for the Aboriginal groups which identify this as their traditional country, including the Gunaikurnai and Boonerwrung people.

Great Ocean Road

OUTSTANDING SCENERY

The Great Ocean Road, which meanders along the south-west coast of Victoria, is considered to be one of the world's great coastal drives. Officially it runs 243 kilometres from Torquay to Allansford, near Warrnambool, but many people choose to continue their journey further to discover the many natural and cultural attractions of Port Fairy, Portland and the surrounds. The road provides access to landmarks such as the Twelve Apostles, as well as some outstanding scenery, including beaches, cliffs, rock formations, temperate rainforest and waterfalls. It also passes through a number of historic seaside towns and villages.

VICTORIA'S SURF COAST

With some of the best surf breaks in the country, the stretch of coastline between Torquay and Apollo Bay is commonly referred to as Victoria's Surf Coast. The famous surf beach, Bells Beach, is located near Torquay, which is renowned as Australia's surfing capital. Each Easter, Bells, as it is affectionately known, hosts the Rip Curl Pro – the world's longest running professional surfing competition – which draws top surfers from all over the globe. Torquay is the home of the Surf World Museum, with an impressive collection of surfing artefacts and memorabilia.

▲ *Great Ocean Road*

GREAT OTWAY NATIONAL PARK

Near Apollo Bay, the road winds inland through Great Otway National Park. Covering much of the Otway Ranges, the park features lush forest, waterfalls and lakes in addition to heathland and rugged coastline and ocean beaches. At Cape Otway stands the Cape Otway Lightstation, the oldest lighthouse in mainland Australia.

THE TWELVE APOSTLES AND OTHER FORMATIONS

Off the shore of Port Campbell National Park are the striking limestone rock stacks of the Twelve Apostles – a widely recognised Australian landmark. The rock formations were

created by the erosion of limestone cliffs, which eventually became caves, then arches, then finally collapsed into the rock stacks that stand today. Previously, there were nine rock stacks but one of them slumped in 2005, leaving just eight standing today. The Twelve Apostles are particularly beautiful at sunrise and sunset.

The Twelve Apostles are not the only spectacular rock formations within Port Campbell National Park and the Bay of Islands Coastal Park. There are many other natural arches, islands, rock stacks and blowholes.

HISTORIC SHIPWRECK TRAIL

There are numerous opportunities for learning about the maritime history of the region, starting with the Historic Shipwreck Trail from Moonlight Bridge in Port Campbell National Park. The wreck of the *Loch Ard* in 1878 is one of the best known incidents. The ship ran aground near Mutton Bird Island. Of the 54 aboard the vessel, only two survivors managed the journey to shore, to the site now known as Loch Ard Gorge, an incredibly beautiful pocket in the coastline. The wreck remains at the base of Mutton Bird Island today.

ABORIGINAL HERITAGE

In addition to great natural beauty, the area has a rich Aboriginal heritage. A number of groups occupied the south-west of the state, including the Gulidjan, Wathaurong, Kirrae Whurrong and Gunditjmara peoples. They continue to have strong cultural and spiritual connections with the country.

Goldfields

GOLD!

The discovery of gold during the 1850s made a lasting impression on the colony of Victoria. News of the finds spread rapidly, attracting immigrants from afar – mostly from Britain, but also from Europe, America and China – in search of their fortune. By 1852 approximately 260 immigrants were arriving in Melbourne each day and tent settlements sprung up in and along the routes to the goldfields to accommodate the new arrivals. Within a short period the temporary facilities were replaced with permanent ones, including houses, shops, grand public buildings, parks and important services and infrastructure.

The goldfields region refers to the central part of Victoria, encompassing the major cities of Ballarat and Bendigo, close to the Mount Alexander goldfield, one of the richest shallow alluvial goldfields in the world, as well as smaller towns, such as Maldon, Castlemaine, Clunes and Creswick.

The legacy of the gold rush is still evident in the region today, with a large number of historic buildings intact. The well-preserved elegant Victorian streetscapes are major tourist draws. Pall Mall, in Bendigo, is particularly impressive.

▲ *Nelson & Wellington Gold Mining Co. print by H. Deutsch*

BALLARAT

In Ballarat, the open-air museum of Sovereign Hill recreates life during the gold rush era. It includes a spectacular re-enactment of the Eureka Rebellion during which goldfield workers clashed with police and military forces on 3 December 1854 over mining licences. Twenty-two diggers and five troopers were killed in the battle. The Eureka Rebellion resulted in a change to the law. It is said to be the first step in Australia becoming a democracy.

BENDIGO

Highlights of Bendigo include the Central Deborah Mine, where visitors can experience a real underground mine, and the 1860s Bendigo Joss House Temple, a place of worship for the region's many Chinese immigrants.

▲ *Old Post Office, Bendigo*

The Grampians

RUGGED BEAUTY

The Grampians, in western Victoria, is an area of outstanding rugged beauty. Within the ancient sandstone mountain ranges there is great diversity, with forests, gullies, cliffs, waterfalls, lakes and wetlands. Surrounded by cleared land, the Grampians provides a refuge for many plant and animal species, including some that are threatened. In addition to the stunning landscapes, there is a strong Aboriginal heritage, including an impressive number of rock art sites.

HISTORY OF THE AREA

The traditional owners, the Djab Wurrung and Jardwadjali people, call the area *Gariwerd*. In 1836 Major Thomas Mitchell, the Surveyor General of New South Wales, visited the area and climbed and named several peaks. The region reminded him of the Grampian Mountains in his native country, Scotland, hence he gave this name to the whole area, elegantly referring to it in his journal as a 'noble range of mountains'. From the 1840s Europeans began to exploit the land for agriculture, mining and logging, and the Djab Wurrung and Jardwadjali people's way of life was severely disrupted.

▶ *Boroka Lookout, Grampians National Park*

ABORIGINAL HERITAGE

The Djab Wurrung and Jardwadjali people shared the land for at least 5000 years prior to European settlement. However, archaeological evidence has indicated the presence of humans in the area from as long as 30,000 years ago. The mountain range, which is central to the Dreaming of the Djab Wurrung and Jardwadjali people, has enormous spiritual and cultural importance to the traditional owners.

Brambuk – the National Park and Cultural Centre in Halls Gap, owned and managed by five Aboriginal communities with traditional connections with the area – is a great place for learning about the natural and cultural history of the region.

The area has been noted for its rock art.

▲ *Eucalyptus trees, Grampians National Park*

DISCOVERY OF GOLD

In 1867 a group of 700 Chinese miners, who were en route to Victoria's Central Goldfields, made the chance discovery of an alluvial goldfield, the Canton Lead. Their find led to the rapid growth of the Ararat goldfield and ultimately the establishment of the town. The Gum San Chinese Heritage Centre, which has been built in a traditional southern Chinese architectural style, reveals more about this episode in the region's history.

GRAMPIANS NATIONAL PARK

Grampians National Park was established in 1984. One of the state's most popular holiday spots, it is ideal for bushwalks, rock climbing and camping. More than 975 plant species – about a third of the state's flora – and 230 bird species have been recorded within the park.

High Country

BEAUTY AND HISTORY

In the north-east of Victoria, in the midst of the beautiful scenery of the Victorian Alps – the highest mountains in the state – is the High Country region. Dotted with vineyards, the area also has significant historical associations, including the discovery of gold and, most famously, as the home of the Kelly Gang.

▲ *Mount Feathertop, Alpine National Park*

STUNNING IN WINTER AND SUMMER

The largest national park in the region is Alpine National Park, which comprises stunning peaks, escarpments, alpine plains, rivers and extensive snow gum forest. The nearby resorts are Mount Buller, Mount Hotham and Falls Creek, the state's largest alpine resort. The north-east corner of the park adjoins Kosciuszko National Park, in New South Wales. Mount Buffalo National Park is the state's oldest national park, declared in 1898, known for its dramatic cliffs and other rock formations. Mount Buffalo is another popular resort. The parks offer a range of recreation options in winter, including skiing, snowboarding and cross-country skiing. In summer the alpine landscapes, abundant with wildflowers, are wonderful places for bushwalking, mountain biking, four-wheel drive touring, camping and fishing, as well as other guided activities. At the foothills of the Victorian Alps is Lake Eildon National Park. The park features the enormous lake of the same name, which was created in the 1950s when the Goulburn River was dammed.

BEECHWORTH – A GOLD RUSH TOWN

The town of Beechworth is known as one of the country's best preserved gold rush towns. Gold was discovered in Beechworth in 1852, with further finds in the surrounding area in the following years, drawing people from afar, particularly Chinese. The town is a popular tourist destination, offering numerous opportunities to learn about early life on the goldfields and the later exploits of the infamous bushranger Ned Kelly. More than 30 National Trust-listed historic buildings, built from granite, stand in the town today.

KELLY COUNTRY

Nearby Glenrowan and Beechworth featured prominently in the story of the bushranger Ned Kelly. In April 1878 Kelly formed a gang of bushrangers, together with his brother Dan and friends Joe Byrne and Steve Hart, after an altercation with a police officer, Constable Alexander Fitzpatrick, at the Kellys' home. The gang hid in nearby bushland while police searched extensively for the men. On 26 October 1878 the gang ambushed and shot dead three policemen, Sergeant Michael Kennedy and Constables Thomas Lonigan and Michael Scanlan. Finally, on 28 June 1880, in a dramatic siege at the Glenrowan Hotel, where the town's people were held hostage, the Kelly Gang was finally brought to justice. All of the members of the gang were killed that day except Kelly, who escaped but was captured soon thereafter. In August that year Ned Kelly's committal hearing was held at the Beechworth Courthouse – now a museum. He was hanged at the Old Melbourne Gaol on 11 November 1880. Glenrowan and Beechworth are part of a touring route through what is commonly referred to as 'Kelly Country'.

▲ *Portrait of Ned Kelly, taken the day before his execution, 1880*

MURRAY RIVER

Australia's longest river, the Murray River, rises in the Australian Alps. It runs for more than 2500 kilometres, forming a large portion of the border between New South Wales and Victoria, before emptying into the ocean via the Murray Mouth in South Australia. The Murray is one of the longest navigable (that is, a river on which boat travel is possible) rivers in the world, third only to the Amazon and Nile rivers.

▲ *Paddlesteamer on the Murray River*

The Murray River is part of the Murray–Darling Basin, a system draining most of the inland parts of New South Wales, the Australian Capital Territory and Victoria as well as parts of Queensland and South Australia. The basin covers a vast area – one seventh of the country's landmass – and provides the habitat for a significant number of native plants and animals.

The Royal Exhibition Building was the largest building in Australia and the highest building in Melbourne when it was built in 1880.

The Great Ocean Road meanders 243 kilometres along the south-west coast of Victoria.

AROUND 638 SHIPS ARE KNOWN TO HAVE BEEN WRECKED ALONG VICTORIA'S COASTLINE, BUT ONLY 240 HAVE BEEN LOCATED.

Cheviot Hill, on the Mornington Peninsula, is named after the SS Cheviot, which struck a reef in the treacherous passage through Port Phillip Bay in 1887. Fifty-six lives were lost in the incident.

At the siege at Glenrowan the Kelly Gang wore suits of armour made from plough parts, iron bolts and leather.

The Murray is Australia's longest river, running for more than 2500 kilometres.

Phillip Island was named after the first Governor of New South Wales, Arthur Phillip.

Grampians National Park has the greatest number of Aboriginal rock art sites in Australia's south-east.

Eureka Tower is Melbourne's tallest building. With 92 levels, it is one of the world's tallest residential buildings.

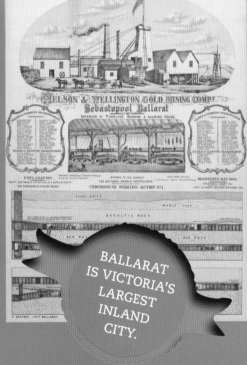

BALLARAT IS VICTORIA'S LARGEST INLAND CITY.

'[...] the most wretched place of involuntary and slavish exilium that can possibly be conceived; nothing could warrant any civilised creature living on such a spot [...]'

Captain Douglass, of the ship *Mariner*, on Macquarie Island, 1822

WESTERn... Phillip... Wonthag... Inverloc... ...rrum

...tch Bay

Cape Wickham

King Island

Grassy

Stokes Point

...unter Island

...lnorth Point

Marrawah
West Point
Hill Point

...dson Point

Arthur...

200

War...

Savage River

TASMANIA

Zeehan

Queenstown
Strahan

Mt O... 161...

Macquarie Harbour

Point Hibbs

Gordon R

Franklin R

River Derwent

Lake Gordon

Tarralea...

Bothwell

Bagdad

Maydena

Strathgordon

New Norfolk

Lake Pedder

Triabunna

...lands

Cape Forestier

Schouten Island

Great Oyster Bay

Bridgewater

Sorell

Maria Island

Low Rocky Point

Mt Picton

Huonville
Geeveston

Cygnet

HOBART
Kingston

Storm Bay

Nubeena
Port Arthur
Cape Pillar

1327

Dover

200

Southport

South West Cape
Maatsuyker Group

Bruny Island
Tasman Head

South East Cape

Hobart

HOBART TOWN

Situated in Tasmania's south-east, Hobart is the state capital and the nation's second oldest capital city after Sydney. The city was established in 1804 by Lieutenant Governor Collins as a penal colony. It was initially called Hobart Town, but by 1881 'Town' was formally dropped from the name. The original penal settlement was based at Risdon Cove in 1803 but was moved the following year to its present site at Sullivans Cove, on the estuary of the Derwent River, which provided better access to the deepwater harbour. This choice led to Hobart's swift development as an international centre for whaling and shipbuilding.

The Flurry c. 1848
William Duke
W. L. Crowther Library
Tasmanian Archive and
Heritage Office

ORIGINAL INHABITANTS

Prior to European settlement, Aboriginal people – the Mouheneener tribe, a sub-group of the Nuennone – had inhabited the area for at least 8000 years. On 3 May 1804 there was a violent encounter between the soldiers at the Risdon Cove settlement and a group of local hunters. The bloody clash resulted in the deaths of between three and 50 Aboriginal people and was one of the first between the British settlers and the Aboriginal inhabitants of the area, tragically with many more to follow over the next two decades. Due to

the hostile conflicts between the two groups, the Aborigines were forced away from their traditional land while disease introduced by the settlers had a further devastating effect on the population. In what is a very sad chapter of Australia's history, by 1830 only 100 of Tasmania's original inhabitants remained. Truganini, who died in 1876, is considered to be the last full-blooded Aboriginal Tasmanian, although this claim has been disputed.

A MAJOR PORT

Today, Hobart remains a major deepwater port in the Southern Ocean and is the departure point for Australian and French expeditions to Antarctica.

▼ *Hobart Harbour*

Hobart is also the finish point of the famous Rolex Sydney Hobart Yacht Race, which starts in Sydney on 26 December each year and ends off Battery Point. The race – approximately 630 nautical miles through extremely challenging conditions – is an important event on the Australian summer sporting calendar.

HERITAGE BUILDINGS

Evidence of Hobart's colonial past is found in the Georgian sandstone buildings along the waterfront and throughout the central business district – along Davey and Macquarie streets alone there are almost 60 National Trust-listed buildings. Among the city's notable heritage buildings are the Commissariat Store, Hobart's oldest public building, which was built between 1808 and 1810 and used to house the colony's supplies; the Penitentiary Chapel historic site, constructed in 1831 as a chapel for the adjoining Prisoner Barracks; and the Theatre Royal, Australia's oldest theatre, built in 1837. Numerous Georgian sandstone waterfront warehouses were built for a variety of purposes between 1830 and 1850 at Salamanca Place, which formed the trading and maritime hub of Hobart.

Linking the Salamanca precinct with Battery Point is a set of steep sandstone stairs called Kelly's Steps. The steps were built in 1840 by James Kelly, an adventurer who circumnavigated Van Diemen's Land, as Tasmania was known until 1856, discovering Port Davey and Macquarie Harbour.

▶ View of wharves looking south by *Anson Brothers, c. 1878, Battery Point, W. L. Crowther Library, Tasmanian Archive and Heritage Office*

BATTERY POINT

Battery Point was one of the first parts of Hobart to be settled. From 1811 free settlers began establishing farms around Battery Point and by the 1830s a range of homes – from tiny cottages to fine mansions – had been built to accommodate workers in various mercantile and maritime occupations. Numerous original colonial, Georgian and Victorian homes can be seen there today.

Another notable location within the suburb is St George's Church, built between 1836 and 1838. It was designed by government architect John Lee Archer in a Neo-Classical style and is one of the most beautiful churches in Hobart. Situated on the highest part of the point, Kermode's Hill, St George's, also known as the 'Mariners' Church', became a landmark for ships.

MOUNT WELLINGTON

Thanks to its location on the foothills of Mount Wellington, a magnificent, 1271-metre-high mountain dominating the city's skyline, Hobart is an attractive city. The mountain is covered in dense forest and frequently also in snow – sometimes even during summer.

▲ *Hobart Harbour with Mount Wellington in the background*

A VIBRANT CITY

Hobart offers a relaxed lifestyle and has a thriving arts scene. Salamanca Market, a weekly outdoor market at Salamanca Place where food, produce and arts and crafts are sold, is a fun, vibrant gathering point for locals and tourists. Until recently the Salamanca Arts Centre and surrounding area was the city's cultural heart. But since 2011, the opening of the Museum of Old and New Art – better known as MONA – on the Berriedale Peninsula, just a short ferry ride from the city, has led to an influx of visitors from mainland Australia – and further ashore – and put Hobart on the map as an important cultural centre.

MONA

A DISTINCTIVE SPACE AND APPROACH TO ART

The Museum of Old and New Art, known as MONA, is an art museum located in Berriedale that has attracted enormous public interest since it opened in January 2011. The museum is the concept of Tasmanian multi-millionaire David Walsh

▲ *Southern facade viewed from Little Frying Pan Island, south of the museum*

and includes more than 400 antiquities and modern and contemporary artworks from his private collection.

The three-level facility, designed by Melbourne architect Nonda Katsalidis, is built into a sandstone cliff overlooking the Derwent River, its underground location reflecting the museum's 'subversive' collection (as Walsh has described it). MONA has led to Hobart's cultural rebirth and contributed to a surge in the state's tourism industry, with visitors flocking from afar to experience the museum's distinctive space and approach.

THE COLLECTION

MONA's collection, comprising installations, paintings and other curiosities – even ancient Egyptian mummies – is intended to push boundaries and even shock visitors. The museum also takes an unconventional approach to the display of works. Instead of labels on the wall, visitors receive a device called an O – an iPod Touch – that can detect their location in relation to the works on display to provide a customised, interactive tour of the space. The O also allows visitors to vote whether they 'love' or 'hate' the artworks and to access their tour later.

▲ *Corten stairwell and surrounding artworks*

Port Arthur Historic Site

TASMANIA'S TOP TOURIST ATTRACTION

The ruins of the former convict settlement of Port Arthur, approximately 60 kilometres south-east of Hobart, are the top tourist attraction in Tasmania. Port Arthur is part of the World Heritage-listed Australian Convict Sites, one of 11 of the country's best examples of our convict history.

▲ *Port Arthur Historic Site*

HISTORY OF THE PENAL STATION

Named after George Arthur, the Lieutenant Governor of Van Diemen's Land, Port Arthur served as a penal station from 1833 to 1877. Located on the isolated Tasman Peninsula, the station was said to be 'inescapable', surrounded by water, supposedly infested with sharks, with the only exit via a narrow isthmus fenced and guarded by soldiers and dogs.

However, numerous prisoners did attempt to flee and some were even successful.

The facility received secondary offenders – those convicts who had committed new crimes following their arrival in the colony. The convicts were set to hard labour, which included felling and sawing timber and quarrying stone. Over time the range of industrial work done at the settlement expanded to include boat- and shipbuilding, the manufacture of clothing and building materials and the operation of a tramway.

Among Port Arthur's prisoner population were juvenile convicts, with boys as young as nine sent to a separate facility at Point Puer. Well-behaved boys were given a basic education, religious instruction and taught trades, while others were assigned to labour.

The discovery of coal on the peninsula led to the establishment of a mine. From 1833 to 1848, convicts worked in the mine, which produced most of Van Diemen's Land's much-needed coal, which had previously been transported from New South Wales. Used as a form of severe punishment, work in the coal mine included digging, quarrying, lime burning and other labour-intensive activities. The Coal Mines Historic Site has been inscribed on the World Heritage List, together with the Port Arthur Historic Site and other significant convict sites.

The Port Arthur prison employed new methods of reform, with a focus on psychological punishment – in the form of separation, intimidation and manipulation – in place

▶ *Central hub of second 'new' prison design, Port Arthur Historic Site*

of the physical punishment dealt out at other penal settlements. Prisoners who behaved well received greater food rations and luxury items, while those who misbehaved got only bread and water. Nonetheless, the prison has been widely criticised as being just as brutal as other penal settlements.

During the 1840s and 1850s, as other penal stations began to close, Port Arthur received an influx of convicts. The transportation of convicts to Van Diemen's Land ended in 1853. Inevitably, the prisoner population became less and less effective with many of the ageing convicts unable to participate in hard labour and a large number suffering from mental illness.

BEYOND THE PRISON DAYS

After the prison's closure in 1877, many of the buildings were demolished. However, it soon became clear that visitors were intrigued about the penal station and, due to continuing public interest, work on its conservation began.

Visitors to Port Arthur can learn the remarkable stories of some of Port Arthur's inhabitants and explore the area.

Tragically, on 28 April 1996, a mass murder took place at the historic site. A sole gunman, Martin Bryant, killed 35 people and wounded 23 others. A memorial garden was created, honouring the victims who lost their lives that day.

▲ *Separate Prison, Port Arthur Historic Site*

A PRISON FOR CONVICT WOMEN

Located at the foothills of Mount Wellington, the Cascades Female Factory was a prison for convict women and their children that operated from 1828 until 1856 – one of the longest running penal institutions in Tasmania. The factory was a major facility for the processing and imprisonment of the penal colony's female convicts.

The Cascades Female Factory's significance – as the only remaining female factory in the country and a place that tells the story of female convicts – has been recognised by its inclusion on both official heritage lists. In August 2007 it was included in the National Heritage List, and in July 2010 it was included on UNESCO's World Heritage List among ten other Australian Convict Sites.

Derwent River

A PICTURESQUE RIVER

The picturesque Derwent River starts at Lake St Clair and flows more than 180 kilometres to Storm Bay through a large estuary which forms Hobart's harbour. At certain points the river is as much as three kilometres across, making it the widest river in Tasmania.

HISTORY OF THE RIVER

▲ *Derwent River in autumn*

The first European to discover the river was the French admiral Bruni d'Entrecasteaux in 1793. D'Entrecasteaux called it *Rivière du Nord*. Just a few months later, the English lieutenant John Hayes explored the area and named the river the Derwent River, after the River Derwent in Cumbria, England. Before the Europeans' arrival, the Aboriginal Mouheneener people lived in the area for approximately 8000 years.

In 1798 Matthew Flinders and George Bass sailed upriver. On their advice, in 1803 Lieutenant John Bowen established the first European settlement on the east bank at Risdon Cove. The following year Lieutenant Governor David Collins moved the settlement to the west bank at Sullivans Cove – Hobart's present location – which was thought to be a superior site.

EXPLOITING THE RIVER

From the colony's beginnings large numbers of whales in the Derwent were noted. Whaling was one of the first industries to be established in Hobart and quickly thrived but by the 1840s whales were scarce due to overexploitation. Fortunately, in recent years, southern right whales have been spotted in the river once again. Many dams and reservoirs have been built on the Derwent's tributaries.

Australian Antarctic Division, Kingston

KEY FACT
HEADQUARTERS OF THE AUSTRALIAN ANTARCTIC DIVISION

PROMOTING AUSTRALIA'S INTERESTS IN ANTARCTICA

Located in Kingston, just south of Hobart – a gateway city to Antarctica – are the Australian Antarctic Division's headquarters. The division is responsible for promoting Australia's strategic, scientific and economic interests in Antarctica, the Southern Ocean and the Subantarctic. Australian territory within the region includes the Australian Antarctic Territory – covering 42 per cent of the Antarctic continent – Heard Island and McDonald Islands and Macquarie Island, and an ongoing presence is required in this area in order to protect Australia's sovereignty. The division also cooperates with other nations with interests in Antarctica to achieve shared goals, and coordinates polar expeditions.

▲ *Sir Douglas Mawson, c. 1930*

The Australian Antarctic Division is an important source of information about Antarctica. The division has three research stations within the Australian Antarctic Territory and one on Macquarie Island, along with remote field bases, which conduct valuable research into the land and marine ecosystems of the Antarctic and the Southern Ocean. A significant part of this work is gaining a better understanding of the consequences of climate change.

Visitors can learn more about the history and science of the Antarctic region in a public display at the Kingston facility.

▼ *Heard Island*

Maria Island

RUGGED BEAUTY OFF TASMANIA'S EAST COAST

Located off Tasmania's east coast, Maria Island ('Maria' is pronounced with an emphasis on the 'i') is a spectacular location with a rich history, from its original Aboriginal inhabitants to two periods as a convict settlement. Now a national park, including a marine nature reserve, the island has abundant flora and fauna and has become a refuge for endangered species.

▶ *Painted Cliffs*

ABORIGINAL HERITAGE

For thousands of years the island was known to local Aboriginal people as *Toarra-marra-monah*. It was part of the land of the Tyreddeme band of the Oyster Bay tribe who regularly canoed across the passage separating the island from the east coast of Tasmania.

EUROPEAN EXPLORERS

In 1642 the island was given the name *Marias Eylandt* (which translates to Maria Island) by the Dutch explorer Abel Tasman. In what was the first European sighting of the island, Tasman named the island after Maria Van Diemen, the wife of Anthony Van Diemen, the Governor-General of the Dutch East India Company, who had sent Tasman on his journey of exploration.

From the 1770s a number of explorers passed by Maria Island, but the first Europeans to come ashore were from the British captain John Henry Cox's brig, HMS *Mercury*, in 1789. (The passage separating Maria Island and Tasmania's east coast is known as Mercury Passage after Cox's ship.) In 1802, a group of French explorers, commanded by Nicolas Baudin, also investigated the island. Both the English and French explorers came into contact with the Aboriginal people on the island.

WHALING HISTORY

The island's early European visitors noted the large numbers of marine life in the waters around Maria Island. From the early 19th century, commercial whaling and sealing began in the area and quickly thrived. Remains of the island's whaling stations still exist. By the 1820s the Aboriginal locals had stopped travelling to Maria Island, most likely due to the whalers' activity.

◀ *Interior of a convict barn*

A WORLD HERITAGE CONVICT SITE

In 1825 a penal settlement was established on the island. Initially, 50 prisoners, together with their guards, arrived at the island but were soon joined by more convicts. The prisoners were put to work developing the new settlement of Darlington. However, the settlement was fraught with problems from the very start. The convicts were in poor health, with many suffering from scurvy, ulcers and boils, and within a short time the first escape from the island had been attempted.

▲ *A convict barn*

As the settlement grew, the convicts were engaged in productive activities, such as weaving, tailoring, carpentry, quarrying, land clearing and building. But the escape attempts continued and discipline was thought to be unsatisfactory. In 1832 the settlement was closed and most of the convicts were sent to Port Arthur.

From 1842 to 1850 Darlington was a probation station. Under the new system of probation, convicts spent a brief period doing hard labour before being allowed to work for wages and ultimately pardoned. During this period numerous buildings were constructed and a second probation station was established on the island in 1845 at Point Lesueur, where the convicts primarily undertook agricultural work.

As one of the most intact examples of a convict probation station, the Darlington Probation Station is considered to be of cultural significance and was recognised on the World Heritage List among the Australian Convict Sites.

▶ *Forester kangaroos on Maria Island*

A STUNNING LANDSCAPE

In 1971 Maria Island was declared a national park. The rugged countryside, including the fascinating, sheer Fossil Cliffs, which contain numerous fossilised sea creatures, and the Painted Cliffs, with stunning patterns stained into the sandstone by iron oxide, is popular with bushwalkers. A number of threatened species, such as Forester kangaroos (also known as eastern grey kangaroos) and Flinders Island wombats, have been introduced to the island. It is also considered one of Tasmania's best spots for birdwatching.

Launceston

GATEWAY TO TASMANIA'S NORTH

Established in 1806, Launceston is the third oldest city in
Australia after Sydney and Hobart and Tasmania's second
largest city. Situated at the point where the North Esk and
South Esk rivers join the Tamar Estuary, Launceston is
an attractive city. It is known for its many well-preserved
historic buildings, its beautiful established parkland and
Cataract Gorge – the main tourist attraction. Launceston's
location in the north of the state makes it a gateway to the
Tamar Valley – a food and wine hotspot – the north-east
coast and, of course, Cradle Mountain.

HISTORY OF LAUNCESTON

Prior to European settlement, the Aboriginal groups who
inhabited the region were known as the Leterremairrener,
Panninher and Tyerrernotepanner peoples.

Explorers George Bass and Matthew Flinders were the first
Europeans to discover the area. In 1798 they were sent to
investigate whether a strait existed between the mainland of
Australia and Van Diemen's Land. They landed in nearby Port
Dalrymple.

In 1804 Lieutenant Colonel William Paterson and his party
established a camp at the present-day site of George Town.
However, within a few weeks, the settlement was relocated
to York Town, and again to Launceston one year later. At first
the settlement was called Patersonia, but Paterson decided to
change the name to Launceston as a tribute to the Governor
of New South Wales, Philip Gidley King, who was born in

▲ *Portrait of Matthew
Flinders, 1814*

◄ *Birdstowe Lavender
Estate Farm, near
Launceston*

Launceston in Cornwall, England. The town quickly grew as a centre for the region's agricultural industry. The population surged with the discovery of first tin and then gold in the region, and in 1888 it was declared a city.

▲ *Town Hall, Launceston*

HISTORIC BUILDINGS

Some of Launceston's outstanding examples of Georgian and Victorian architecture include Franklin House, built in 1838, the birthplace of the National Trust in Tasmania; Custom House, constructed in 1885; the post office, built in the late 1880s; and Albert Hall, completed in 1891.

CATARACT GORGE

Just a 15-minute walk from the city centre, Cataract Gorge is a spectacular natural formation. Visitors can experience breathtaking views of the South Esk River from a number of lookouts, a suspension bridge and a chairlift – thought to be the world's longest single-span chairlift. The Duck Reach Power Station was the first municipal hydro-electric power station in Australia. The plant provided Launceston with hydro-electric power from 1895 to 1955, when it could no longer adequately meet the city's needs.

BRICKENDON AND WOOLMERS ESTATES

Approximately 20 kilometres from Launceston, near Longford, are Brickendon and Woolmers estates, adjoining farming properties that have been held in continuous operation by six generations of the Archer family, beginning in the early 19th century. The farming properties, considered to be the most significant rural estates in the nation, provide insight into the experience of colonial settlers and the convicts assigned to rural estates. Brickendon Estate and Woolmers Estate shared resources, with a combined convict assignment of more than 100. The properties were included on the National Heritage List in 2007. In 2010 Brickendon Estate and Woolmers Estate were jointly listed as a World Heritage Site, one of 11 World Heritage Australian Convict Sites.

▲ *Outbuildings at Woolmers Estate*

Cradle Mountain –Lake St Clair National Park

INCREDIBLE NATURAL BEAUTY

The Cradle Mountain–Lake St Clair National Park, located in the Central Highlands, comprises part of Tasmania's World Heritage-listed Wilderness Area. The national park, which covers roughly 1610 square kilometres, is renowned for its natural beauty. Cradle Mountain, a spectacular jagged mountain at the park's northern end, is one of the main tourist destinations in the state. Rising 1545 metres above sea level, the mountain offers stunning views of the park, including Dove Lake, which was formed by glaciation. Tasmania's highest mountain, Mount Ossa, reaching 1617 metres above sea level, is also found in the national park.

MOUNTAIN CLIMBING AND WALKING

The park is popular with climbers and walkers. The Overland Track, a challenging 65-kilometre trek through magnificent mountainous terrain, is one of Australia's most famous

◄ *Cradle Mountain—Lake St Clair National Park*

▶ *Cradle Mountain and Dove Lake*

▲ *Flowering heath in Walls of Jerusalem National Park*

bushwalks. It starts at Cradle Mountain and ends at Lake St Clair – the deepest lake in the country, with a maximum depth of 167 metres – and takes approximately six days.

SIGNIFICANT FLORA AND FAUNA

The vegetation in the area is diverse, including ancient cool temperate rainforest, eucalypt forest, grassland and alpine meadows. Many of the flora species are endemic to Tasmania – that is, they are only found there – and some date back to Gondwanan times. The fauna includes Tasmanian devils, quolls, platypus and echidnas.

It was thanks to the dedication of Austrian immigrant Gustav Weindorfer that the area was declared a scenic reserve in 1922.

The spectacular Walls of Jerusalem National Park, which also forms part of the Tasmanian Wilderness World Heritage Area, sits on the Cradle Mountain–Lake St Clair National Park's eastern boundary.

TASMANIAN WILDERNESS

▲ *Tasman Arch*

The Tasmanian Wilderness Area covers approximately 20 per cent of the island of Tasmania. The Tasmanian Wilderness was included on the World Heritage List in 1982, recognised as having both natural and cultural values of global significance. The area conserves one of the last remaining wilderness regions on the planet. It is home to some of the oldest trees and tallest flowering plants and provides the habitat for several animals that are endangered or have become extinct on mainland Australia. Aboriginal occupation of the area dates back as far as 45,000 years. Limestone caves in the region contain some of the earliest forms of art. A number of sites within the Wilderness Area have been returned to Tasmania's Aboriginal community.

Macquarie Island

A REMOTE, INHOSPITABLE PLACE

Approximately 1500 kilometres south-east of Tasmania, about halfway between Australia and Antarctica, sits Macquarie Island. Macquarie Island is long and narrow: 34 kilometres long and approximately five kilometres across at its widest point. Conditions on the remote island are unwelcoming: it is cold, windy and wet. It rains for more than 300 days a year and snow can even fall in the summer months.

On 3 December 1997 the island was declared a World Heritage Site because of its geological characteristics and extraordinary natural diversity. Macquarie Island is a rare example – in fact, the only known place – where the oceanic crust has been pushed above sea level. It is a breeding ground for the Southern Ocean's animals and birds – one of only a few locations in the Pacific part of the Southern Ocean where animals can breed. Each year approximately 3.5 million birds and 80,000 elephant seals come to the island.

HISTORY OF THE ISLAND

The remote island was discovered accidentally on 11 July 1810 by Captain Frederick Hasselborough while on a sealing trip. Hasselborough reported seeing a wreck 'of ancient design' on the island, which suggests that perhaps Polynesians were there before him. He named the island after the Governor of New South Wales, Lachlan Macquarie. The island was initially declared to be part of New South Wales but in 1890 was transferred to the state of Tasmania. It was immediately dismissed as a possible location for a penal settlement due to the unfavourable climate.

EXPLOITING THE ISLAND

Although Macquarie Island would prove to be an important discovery for both geological and ecological reasons, in the early 19th century many focused only on the island's huge

▲ *King penguins on the island*

seal population – initially estimated to be between 200,000 and 400,000. Commercial sealing began and within ten years the fur seals had almost disappeared. The sealers then set their sights on the Macquarie Island's elephant seal and royal penguin populations. Commercial activities around the island ceased in 1920.

Another devastating effect of the sealers' presence on Macquarie Island's ecology was the accidental introduction of rats and mice from the ships. The rodents thrived due to a lack of predators. Cats were then introduced to control the rats, but they also threatened the native seabird population. Rabbits were also brought by the sealers to create a food supply. They too quickly multiplied and attacked the young chicks and caused severe erosion on the island.

A PLACE OF SCIENTIFIC INTEREST

From the time of its discovery, Macquarie Island was a place of great scientific interest, with numerous expeditions made to the island over the years. Notably, scientists travelling with famous British explorers Captain Robert Scott, in 1901, and Sir Ernest Shackleton, in 1909, collected specimens on the island.

The island's first scientific station was established by the Australian explorer Sir Douglas Mawson in 1911. Extensive studies were carried out, including mapping the island, geomagnetic observations and research into Macquarie Island's botany, zoology, geology and meteorology. Mawson's Australasian Antarctic Expedition also established the first radio link between Australia and Antarctica via a radio relay station on Wireless Hill.

▼ Left: *Aurora australis above the Australian Antarctic Division's Macquarie Island station*
▼ Right: *Sir Douglas Mawson at Caroline Cove, Macquarie Island as part of the Australasian Antarctic Expedition, 1911–1914*

In 1948 a permanent research station was founded on the island at Buckles Bay and has been operating ever since. Its staff are the only human inhabitants of the island.

A WILDLIFE SANCTUARY

Macquarie Island was declared a wildlife sanctuary in 1933 and later a conservation area. The island and its surrounds now form part of the Macquarie Island Nature Reserve (1978) and the Macquarie Island Commonwealth Marine Reserve (1999). In recent years, Macquarie Island's pests have been almost completely eradicated, allowing the bird populations to flourish once more. Fur seals are also increasing in numbers after almost disappearing completely due to overexploitation.

◀ *Elephant seals and king penguins on the island*

ONE OF THE MOST STRIKING PIECES IN MONA'S COLLECTION AT THE TIME OF OPENING WAS SIR SIDNEY NOLAN'S SNAKE MURAL, 45 METRES LONG AND COMPOSED OF 1620 INDIVIDUAL PAINTINGS, WHICH HAS RARELY BEEN ON DISPLAY.

Maria Island is in fact two islands joined by a narrow sandy bar called McRaes Isthmus.

Port Arthur was the British Government's last penal settlement in Australia.

Launceston is Australia's third oldest city. It is a gateway for the stunning Tamar Valley and Cradle Mountain, part of Tasmania's World Heritage-listed Wilderness Area.

'Storm Boy lived between the Coorong and the sea [...] A wild strip it is, windswept and tussocky, with the flat shallow water of the South Australian Coorong on one side and the endless slam of the Southern Ocean on the other.'

Colin Thiele, *Storm Boy*, set on the Coorong

SOUTH AUSTRALIA

Adelaide

A VIBRANT CAPITAL

With a population of just over 1 million, Adelaide ranks as Australia's fifth largest city but makes up for its comparatively small size with a vibrant culture. It is home to numerous arts festivals, including the Adelaide Festival, the Adelaide Fringe Festival and WOMADelaide, a music and dance festival. The city also hosts several major sporting events, such as the Santos Tour Down Under, a cycling event that draws some of the biggest names in the sport; the Clipsal 500, a V8 Super Cars event; and the World Tennis Challenge.

▲ Adelaide and the Torrens River

AN ELEGANT PLACE

Adelaide has a reputation as an elegant place, with many fine examples of colonial architecture, and parkland covering 45 per cent of the city. It is also touted as having a fantastic lifestyle centred on coastal living and gourmet food and wine experiences. In recent years, Adelaide has consistently ranked in the top ten of the Economist Intelligent Unit's index of the world's most liveable cities (City Liveability Index).

HISTORY OF ADELAIDE

The original inhabitants of the Adelaide Plains were the Kaurna people. In recent times, the Adelaide City Council has sought to acknowledge this Aboriginal heritage through the use of Kaurna placenames across the city. In 2001 the River Torrens was given the dual name of *Karrawirra Parri*, meaning 'river of the redgum forests', the original Kaurna name for the river.

Adelaide was proclaimed as a new British colony on 28 December 1836. Unlike the penal settlements of Sydney, Brisbane and Hobart, it would be a place for free immigrants. It was in fact the second attempt at establishing a free settlement in Australia – a settlement at Reeves Point on Kangaroo Island was abandoned in preference for the mainland due to insufficient natural resources.

Situated north of the Fleurieu Peninsula, Adelaide sits on the Adelaide Plains and is flanked by the Mount Lofty Ranges. The city extends from the coast to the foothills of the ranges. A significant feature of the Adelaide Plains which contributed to the decision to move the colony from Kangaroo Island was the River Torrens. The city was planned by Colonel William Light, South Australia's first Surveyor General, in a grid layout with wide streets and extensive parkland. It was the nation's first planned city.

▲ *View of Adelaide, c. 1890*

ADELAIDE TODAY

Today Adelaide is surrounded by gardens and parks. The Adelaide Botanic Gardens, which were part of Colonel Light's original plan for the city, opened in 1857 and draw more than 1 million visitors each year. Several significant Victorian garden buildings are situated within the grounds. The city is known for its beautiful, vivid rose gardens, such as those found in Rymill Park and Veale Gardens. Some of the city's gardens have a distinctive character. In 2008 the Park Lands and layout of the City of Adelaide were named on the National Heritage List.

CITY OF CHURCHES

Adelaide is often referred to as the 'City of Churches', a name given to the city as early as the mid 19th century. Adelaide's churches are among the oldest buildings in the city. Notable examples include Holy Trinity, on North Terrace, which was the city's first church, built in 1838, and the Quaker Meeting House, on Pennington Terrace, built in 1840.

ADELAIDE'S ATTRACTIONS

One of Adelaide's main attractions is the beachside suburb of Glenelg, which was the colony's original site. Set on the shores of Holdfast Bay, many of the city's tourists choose to stay in Glenelg, a hub for entertainment and dining. The suburb has a long history as a recreation centre, with several amusement parks located there since the 1930s. The Glenelg

▲ *Glenelg Jetty, Adelaide*

Jetty – originally built in 1859 but rebuilt in 1969 – is a famous city landmark. The Glenelg Tram, connecting the CBD and Glenelg, is now the city's only operating tram service. The vintage 1929 H-class tram cars are an icon of the city.

One of the city's most popular institutions is the Bradman Collection at the Adelaide Oval, which houses an impressive selection of memorabilia bequeathed to South Australia by Sir Donald Bradman. Adelaide also hosts an important cultural institution known as Tandanya, the National Aboriginal Cultural Institute, a multi-arts centre at which visitors can learn more about Australia's Aboriginal and Torres Strait Islander culture.

The Adelaide Central Market is another of the city's icons, running for more than 140 years. There are over 80 stalls, selling a wide range of fruit, vegetables, meat, poultry, seafood and gourmet produces, attracting approximately 1 million visitors each month.

PORT ADELAIDE

Fourteen kilometres from Adelaide City is Port Adelaide, the city's main port, which was founded in 1837. It served as a hub for the state's trade and commerce. All new arrivals to the colony also disembarked there. Port Adelaide has many fine examples of colonial and Victorian architecture and was the first area in the state to be named a heritage precinct.

Adelaide Hills

A MAJOR TOURIST DESTINATION

To the east of Adelaide are the Adelaide Hills, which are part of the Mount Lofty Ranges and a major South Australian tourist destination, with many visitors drawn to the area's picturesque historic towns and villages. The Adelaide Hills are also renowned as a wine region, producing fine cool-climate wines. The area has also developed a reputation as a gourmet food spot.

HISTORY OF THE HILLS

The Adelaide Hills was one of the first parts of South Australia to be settled by Europeans. However, the Peramangk, Kaurna and Ngarrindjeri people had lived in or visited the area for at least 2400 years.

Hahndorf was the first settlement in Australia intended for non-British immigrants. On 28 December 1838 the ship *Zebra* came into Port Adelaide, carrying a group of German Lutheran immigrants. The captain, Dirk Hahn, helped to negotiate land for the passengers on their arrival. The settlement was called Hahndorf, which means 'Hahn's village', in honour of Captain Hahn. Today, Hahndorf and other parts of the Adelaide Hills have retained a distinctly German character, reflected in the architecture, schools, churches and retail outlets.

SIR HANS HEYSEN

One of the area's most famous residents was Sir Hans Heysen, an Australian artist who was born in 1877 in Germany but migrated to Adelaide when he was six. Heysen became widely known for his paintings of Australian landscapes and farming scenes and won the prestigious Wynne prize nine times. Heysen developed a love of the Adelaide Hills countryside, which was the subject of many of his works. In 1912 he purchased a property called The Cedars, near Hahndorf, where he lived and worked until his death in 1968. The Cedars is still owned by his family and visitors can tour his studio.

▲ The hill of the creeping shadow *1929*
Hans Heysen
oil on canvas, 66 x 92 cm
Art Gallery of New South Wales
Photo: AGNSW
© C Heysen

THE REGION'S ATTRACTIONS

Stirling is an attractive town in the region. It was settled in the 1880s as a centre for apple growing and market gardening. Some of Adelaide's wealthiest people built summer houses – some were, in fact, grand mansions – in the area to escape the heat of the city. The town's many deciduous trees, imported from Europe, are spectacular in autumn.

The Mount Lofty summit is a compelling feature of the area. It rises 710 metres above sea level and offers panoramic views of Adelaide and the coast. On clear days Kangaroo Island can be seen. Mount Barker is the biggest town in the Adelaide Hills, located at the base of a peak with the same name. The summit of Mount Barker is an important Aboriginal site.

▲ *Bunches of blue grapes at a Barossa Valley vineyard*

A TOP WINE-PRODUCING REGION

South Australia is dotted with wineries – in fact, it is the largest national producer of wine, making half of Australia's output. There are 18 recognised grape-growing areas in South Australia, some of the best known being the Clare Valley, the Barossa Valley, the Adelaide Hills, McLaren Vale and the Coonawarra. A great range of wines is produced by South Australia's wineries, due to the variation in climate and geography across the whole region. The Barossa Valley is one of Australia's most famous wine areas and a major tourist destination.

Flinders Ranges

AN IMPORTANT, BEAUTIFUL AREA

The Flinders Ranges has the distinction of being South Australia's largest mountain range, extending more than 430 kilometres from Crystal Brook, near Port Pirie, to Lake Callabonna, but of greater significance are the geology, the ecology and the cultural heritage of the area.

The Flinders Ranges is a stunning landscape of peaks, ridges and gorges that are abundant with plant and animal life. The focal point of the Flinders Ranges is Wilpena Pound, an enormous, and quite magnificent, bowl-shaped geological formation, often likened to a natural amphitheatre. Wilpena Pound is almost completely surrounded by two mountain ranges. St Mary Peak is the highest peak in the walls of Wilpena Pound, and indeed the Flinders Ranges itself, reaching 1170 metres.

THE TRADITIONAL OWNERS

The traditional owners of the land are the Adnyamathanha people. Many of the physical features of the Flinders Ranges have great meaning for them, which has been expressed through songlines and rock art, including at Yourambulla Caves, Sacred Canyon and Arkaroo Rock in Wilpena. *Ikara*, which is the name the Adnyamathanha have given to Wilpena Pound, meaning 'meeting place', is an especially sacred site.

In 2009 the Adnyamathanha were granted native title over 41,000 square kilometres of land, including Flinders Ranges National Park.

▲ *Flinders Ranges*

EUROPEAN EXPLORATION

In 1802 the first Europeans to sight the region were Matthew Flinders and his crew on board HMS *Investigator*. Flinders sent several of his crew to explore the area, naming Mount Brown. In 1839 Edward John Eyre travelled through the range on the first of several attempts to explore Central Australia. The Governor of South Australia at the time, Governor Gawler, named the range after Flinders.

▲ *Matthew Flinders*

DIVERSE FLORA AND FAUNA

A wide variety of plant and animal life is found throughout the Flinders Ranges. More than half of South Australia's plant species are present, ranging from mallee to ferns. The area is known in particular for yellow-footed rock wallabies – which have attractive yellow, brown, black, grey and white markings on their bodies. More than 100 native bird species, such as emus, parrots, galahs and wedge-tailed eagles, are found in this region.

A SIGNIFICANT ARCHAEOLOGICAL SITE

The Flinders Ranges is a very important archaeological site. In 1946 geologist Reginald Sprigg discovered a wealth of fossil imprints of soft-bodied creatures dating from between 570 and 540 million years ago – when much of eastern Australia was under water – in the Ediacara Hills of the Flinders Ranges. Although they were not the first fossils of ancient multi-celled organisms ever to be discovered, their diversity and condition was impressive. One of these organisms has been named *Spriggina*, in Sprigg's honour, and the geological period from 635 million to 542 million years ago has been designated the Ediacaran Period, after the location in which the fossils were found. The discovery was groundbreaking for two reasons: it was the first new geological period to be identified in more than a century; and also, until then, scientists believed that only organisms with hard body parts could be preserved as fossils.

▶ *Wilpena Pound, Flinders Ranges*

FLINDERS RANGES TRAILS

Two famous trails – the Heysen Trail and Mawson Trail – pass through the Flinders Ranges, attracting numerous bushwalkers and cyclists each year.

Kangaroo Island

KEY FACT
SOUTH
AUSTRALIA'S
FIRST FORMAL
SETTLEMENT

A MAJOR TOURIST DESTINATION

Located 110 kilometres south-east of Adelaide, Kangaroo Island is a major South Australian and national tourist destination. It is Australia's third largest island – 155 kilometres long and 50 kilometres wide, covering an area of approximately 4400 square kilometres.

▲ *West Bay*

HISTORY OF THE ISLAND

The island has a fascinating history. It was once part of mainland Australia but became isolated about 10,000 years ago as the sea levels rose. Archaeological evidence of stone tools and campsites has suggested that Aboriginal people inhabited the land as far back as 16,000 years ago, before its separation from the mainland, and as recently as 2000 years ago, after its separation from the mainland. The mainland Aboriginal tribes called the island *Karta*, or 'island of the dead'.

On 22 March 1802 British explorer Captain Matthew Flinders arrived at the island on HMS *Investigator* and disembarked on the north coast. He named the island 'Kangaroo Island' after the abundant supply of kangaroos, which were much welcomed by the ship's hungry crew.

▲ *Sketch of grass trees on Kangaroo Island, c. 1865*

He also named the strait between Kangaroo Island and the mainland 'Backstairs Passage'. On 8 April 1802 Flinders met with the French ship *Le Géographe*, captained by Nicolas Baudin. The French commander went on to circumnavigate and map most of the island's coastline and many of the island's places still have French names today.

At first, Kangaroo Island attracted sealers, escaped convicts and sailors and, in a shameful piece of Australian history, a number of kidnapped Aboriginal women from Tasmania and South Australia were also brought there. The first official settlers arrived on the island on 27 July 1836 via the British ship the *Duke of York* – making it South Australia's first formal settlement. Due to the island's inadequate natural resources, the settlement at Reeves Point, on Kangaroo Island, was abandoned in favour of mainland South Australia. The initial European settlers on the island did not find evidence of the previous Aboriginal inhabitants – it was only in the 1900s that Aboriginal artefacts were found.

Over the years the island was developed as an agricultural centre, producing wool, meat, grain, wine, honey and lobsters. But its greatest success has been tourism, and each year more than 140,000 people from

▶ *Remarkable Rocks*

Australia and overseas visit the island to soak up its great natural beauty, spot the wildlife, enjoy the local produce and delve into its rich history.

NATURAL BEAUTY

Thanks to the island's isolation, the effects of European settlement have been less devastating on the ecology than in other parts of the country. More than a third of the island has been designated as national or conservation parks or wilderness areas. The largest of these is Flinders Chase National Park, the location of two spectacular rock formations shaped by weathering and erosion: Remarkable Rocks, ancient giant boulders, and Admirals Arch, a natural rock arch. The landscape is diverse, with forest, wetlands, sand dunes, cliffs, secluded coves and pristine white-sand beaches.

▲ *Cape du Couedic Lighthouse*

With a lack of introduced predators, the island has a number of plant and animal species that are threatened elsewhere or are endemic, that is, they are found nowhere else. The island even has its own species of kangaroo: the Kangaroo Island kangaroo, a subspecies of the western grey kangaroo.

HISTORIC PLACES

The island has several historically significant places, such as Reeves Point, the site of the first European settlement, and Prospect Hill, which Matthew Flinders climbed in order to survey the island. Kangaroo Island also features the first lighthouse to be built in South Australia, in 1852 at Cape Willoughby, with two more, at Cape Borda and Cape du Couedic, constructed later. The various lighthouses offer magnificent views of the surrounding landscape and sea and are popular tourist attractions, but served an important role in guiding ships in the vicinity through difficult conditions. Since the island's settlement in 1836 more than 80 maritime vessels have been wrecked off the coast of Kangaroo Island, with some resulting in the loss of human life. The most tragic incident occurred in 1905 when the *Loch Vennachar* sailed into rocks on the west coast and claimed 27 lives. A site on the island, Vennachar Point, was named in tribute to the ship's crew and the Cape du Couedic Lighthouse was constructed soon thereafter.

The Coorong, Lower Lakes and Murray Mouth

IMPORTANT WETLANDS

The Coorong, Lower Lakes and Murray Mouth region covers an area of more than 140,000 hectares and consists of numerous important wetlands. The Murray Mouth is the end point of Australia's longest and largest river, the Murray. The mouth sits between two peninsulas – Sir Richard Peninsula, to the north-west, and Younghusband Peninsula, to the south-west. On the north-west side a row of islands divides the Murray Mouth from Lake Alexandrina – the largest of the Murray Lakes. Hindmarsh Island is the biggest of these islands, with the distinctive feature of having salt water on one shore and fresh water on the other. On the south-west side of the Murray Mouth, a shallow saltwater lagoon, called the Coorong, extends 130 kilometres, partitioned from the Southern Ocean by Younghusband Peninsula. The Lower Lakes, including Lake Alexandrina and Lake Albert, are freshwater lakes. Historically, the lakes were composed of mostly fresh water but received some inflows of salt water from tides and storms. A series of barrages were built during the 1930s to prevent saline water from the Murray Mouth and Coorong lagoon from entering the lakes and river.

The region provides a range of habitats for large numbers of waterbirds and many other plant and animal species, including some threatened or endangered species, such as the Murray cod and the orange-bellied parrot. The area also supports migratory birds; in total, 23 different wetland types are represented. In 1985 it was listed under the Ramsar Convention on Wetlands of International Importance.

Over the years enormous pressure has been placed on the Murray River system, with water being extracted for irrigation and to supply regional towns. In recent years reduced river flows to the Coorong, Lower Lakes and Murray Mouth area have resulted in serious environmental stress. A management plan is in place to try to protect this extremely valuable site.

CULTURAL HERITAGE

The region is also a place of tremendous cultural significance. The Ngarrindjeri people, who are made up of 18 tribes, are the traditional owners of the land and adjacent water. They have a strong relationship with the area, which is known as *Yarluwar-Ruwe*, or sea country. Archaeological sites have shown Aboriginal occupation of the area over tens of thousands of years, and it supported the highest density Aboriginal population in Australia before the Europeans arrived. Particular sites, animals and plants within the area have great cultural and spiritual meaning to the Ngarrindjeri people and they have played an active role in managing and conserving the local environment.

▼ *River Murray*

Nullarbor Plain

A VAST PLAIN

The Nullarbor Plain stretches all the way from Ceduna in South Australia to Norseman in Western Australia – a distance of approximately 1100 kilometres. It covers a vast area of 270,000 square kilometres, with one third in South Australia and two thirds in Western Australia. To the north of the Nullarbor is the Great Victoria Desert and to the south is the Great Australian Bight, a well-recognised indentation in the coastline of southern Australia.

▶ *Great Australian Bight*

A KARST LANDSCAPE

It is the world's largest limestone karst – a geological formation produced by the dissolution of layers of soluble rock. Throughout the Nullarbor Plain extensive underground cave systems, sinkholes, known as dolines, and blowholes are found – typical features of karst landscapes. Some of the caves stretch deep below the land's surface and are filled with water. Most of the caves are inaccessible to the public.

The Nullabor's caves are of both archaeological and cultural significance. A wealth of ancient fossils, between 0.5 and 1 million years old, has been discovered in the caves beneath the Nullarbor Plain in recent years. The fossil finds include skeletons and bones of megafauna – long-extinct animals, such as the Thylacoleo, Australia's marsupial 'lion', as well as giant wombats and short-faced kangaroos.

The Murrawijinie Caves – some of the area's best known caves – feature ancient hand stencils. Koonalda Cave is another important cave site, which reveals finger markings on the walls dating from more than 20,000 years ago. The cave was also used by Aboriginal people as a flint mine. (Flint was used to make early tools.) Many of the caves have cultural and spiritual significance for the Aboriginal groups with connections to the Nullarbor region. (A number of semi-nomadic people inhabited the area.)

HISTORY OF THE PLAIN

Edward John Eyre was the first European to cross the Nullarbor Plain, travelling from Adelaide, in South Australia, to Albany, in Western Australia, between 1840 and 1841. The difficult journey – during which Eyre and his team suffered numerous setbacks – is one of the great stories of Australian exploration.

The surveyor Edward Alfred Delisser named the plain in 1865. 'Nullarbor' is said to come from the Latin words *nullus* (no) and *arbor* (tree), hence 'no trees', and indeed much of the landscape is treeless. However, vegetation is present, mostly in the forms of saltbush, bluebush and some mallee. Much of the land is protected by the Nullarbor National Park and Reserve.

RENOWNED DRIVING ROUTE

The Nullarbor Plain has Australia's longest straight section of sealed road. Driving across the Nullarbor has become popular both with international tourists and Australians seeking an 'Outback' experience.

▲ *Perth Museum acting curator Duncan Merrilees holding the skull of a Tasmanian wolf found in a cave on Nullabor Plain, 1965*

◄ *Eyre Highway*

Coober Pedy

'OPAL CAPITAL OF THE WORLD'

The Outback town of Coober Pedy lies approximately 850 kilometres north of Adelaide and 690 kilometres south of Alice Springs. In 1915 opal was discovered in Coober Pedy. Within a short time the miners had moved in. It is now the world's largest producer of opals, with more than 70 opal fields covering almost 5000 square kilometres. For this reason it is sometimes called the 'opal capital of the world'. With residents from more than 40 countries, Coober Pedy is one of Australia's most multicultural locations, owing to its opal mining history.

▲ Coober Pedy

HISTORY OF COOBER PEDY

The area was occupied by Aboriginal people for many years prior to European settlement. It is generally recognised as the traditional country of the Antakirinja Matu-Yankunytjatjara people, but other groups also have connections with the area.

Initially the town was named the Stuart Range Opal Field, in honour of John McDouall Stuart, who was the first European to explore the region. It was renamed Coober Pedy in 1920 – an anglicised version of the Aboriginal terms *kupa* and *piti*, which have been roughly translated as 'white man's hole'.

DUGOUTS

Coober Pedy is famous for its underground dwellings, called 'dugouts', which provide comfortable temperatures in an area that experiences both extreme heat and cold. The original dugouts were very basic but the contemporary ones have all modern conveniences and can be quite luxurious.

ATTRACTIONS OF THE AREA

▲ The Breakaways

Two natural attractions of the area include Moon Plain, an expansive rocky landscape said to resemble the moon's surface, and the Breakaways, a series of colourful rock formations. The locations have been featured in a number of films. The Breakaways, among other sites, have much significance for the traditional owners.

Oodnadatta

A REMOTE TOWN WITH A RICH HISTORY

Located 1000 kilometres north of Adelaide is the small town of Oodnadatta, which has the distinction of having recorded the hottest temperature in Australia: 50.7°C in 1960. It is one of the hottest and driest places in the country. The town can be accessed via two dirt roads, Oodnadatta Road, between Oodnadatta and Coober Pedy, or the historic Oodnadatta Track, which is one of Australia's most famous Outback trails.

THE OODNADATTA TRACK

The track was a traditional route taken by Aboriginal traders transporting materials between the Flinders Ranges and Central Australia and was also used for ceremonies. The route through the arid country was possible due to natural springs seeping up from the Great Artesian Basin, an enormous underground water reservoir. These oases are still found at numerous points along the track and for this reason it is sometimes referred to as the 'String of Springs'. The Overland Telegraph Line, which stretched from Port Augusta to Darwin, was built along the track in 1872, enabling Australia to communicate with the rest of the world.

▲ *Camels beside the Oodnadatta Track*

From the late 1860s the route was used by camel teams, led by drivers brought from Afghanistan, to carry goods within Central Australia. Camels were the only pack animal that could withstand the hot, dry conditions. Oodnadatta was the terminus of a railway line, called the Great Northern Railway, which operated out of Adelaide from 1891. It wasn't until 1929 that a link to Alice Springs was built. The train service soon became known as *The Afghan Express*, shortened to *The Ghan*, after the Afghan camel drivers.

▼ *Oodnadatta Track, c. 1928*

Lake Eyre

SPECTACULAR, DRY OR FLOODED

Lake Eyre fills to capacity only a couple of times a century and when it does, it is Australia's largest lake. It is also the lowest point in Australia, sitting 15 metres below sea level. The lake is spectacular whether dry or flooded. When it is empty, its surface is covered in a crystalline salt crust, which has been formed from the evaporation of floodwaters over thousands of years. When the lake floods – which happens about once every eight years – either from its catchment areas, primarily the Warburton River, or heavy local rainfall, the salt crust starts to dissolve.

Lake Eyre is the lowest point in the Lake Eyre Basin, an enormous drainage basin that covers approximately 1,140,000 square kilometres – almost one sixth of the Australian continent. The basin extends across parts of South Australia, the Northern Territory, Queensland and New South Wales. It is one of the largest internally draining systems in the world. (In other words, the river systems drain inland rather than towards the sea.)

▶ *Lake Eyre (dry)*

THE LAKE IN FLOOD

Lake Eyre in times of flood is an incredible sight, attracting waterbirds in huge numbers. It has been named a BirdLife International Important Bird Area for its role in hosting major breeding events of banded stilts and Australian pelicans, as well as more than one per cent of the global populations of silver gulls, red-necked avocets, sharp-tailed sandpipers, red-necked stints and Caspian terns. During times of flood, the lake contains several species of freshwater fish that can tolerate varying degrees of salinity, such as the Lake Eyre hardyhead and bony bream, but as the salinity rises, the fish die and brine shrimp begin to hatch and breed.

◀ *Lake Eyre (filled)*

HISTORY OF THE LAKE

The lake is named after explorer Edward John Eyre, who was the first European to sight it, in 1840. The lake has two sections, Lake Eyre North and Lake Eyre South. Lake Eyre North was originally thought to be permanently dry. There were occasional reports of sightings of water in the lake, but these were said to be mistaken. It was only in 1949, the first recorded filling of the lake, that it became clear that Lake Eyre North did at times hold water.

Lake Eyre and its surrounds – an area of about 13,500 square kilometres – were declared a national park in 1985.

THE TRADITIONAL OWNERS

In a landmark case in 2012, the Federal Court granted the land's traditional owners, the Arabana, native title to more than 68,000 square kilometres in northern South Australia, including Lake Eyre, which has great meaning for the Arabana. Native title gives the Arabana unconditional access to the lake and surrounding area for hunting, camping, fishing and traditional ceremonies. The lake is now officially known as Kati Thanda–Lake Eyre in recognition of the name used by the Arabana.

The Nullarbor Plain is credited as having the longest straight section of railway, 478 kilometres in total, in the world.

Oodnadatta provides access to the Simpson Desert, Australia's fourth largest desert, which straddles South Australia, Queensland and the Northern Territory.

THE BAROSSA VALLEY HAS A HISTORY OF GRAPE GROWING AND WINEMAKING STRETCHING BACK MORE THAN 150 YEARS.

From the 1920s to the 1940s esteemed artist Sir Hans Heysen travelled on numerous occasions to the Flinders Ranges to study the landscape. His sketches formed the basis of his paintings.

A 14-year-old boy by the name of Willie Hutchinson found the first opals in the Coober Pedy area while looking for gold with his father.

Lake Eyre gained international attention in 1964 as the site where Donald Campbell set a world land speed record.

ON CLEAR DAYS YOU CAN SEE MOUNT LOFTY IN THE DISTANT ADELAIDE HILLS FROM KANGAROO ISLAND.

The Flinders Ranges is South Australia's largest mountain range.

HAHNDORF'S NAME WAS CHANGED TO AMBLESIDE DUE TO ANTI-GERMAN SENTIMENT DURING WORLD WAR I. IN 1935 IT WAS CHANGED BACK TO HAHNDORF.

Australian author Colin Thiele's book, *Storm Boy* (1964) was adapted into a successful film and is set in the Coorong.

'The frenzy at Cape Cuvier, the presence of the whale sharks at Exmouth and [...] the dolphins at Monkey Mia are barely understood phenomena, but ones which must be regarded as privileges to behold.'

Tim Winton, *Land's Edge: A Coastal Memoir*, on Ningaloo Reef

Perth

A STRIKING, COSMOPOLITAN CITY

With a population of just under 2 million, Perth ranks as the nation's fourth largest city, but due to the recent Western Australian mining boom, it is the fastest growing capital city (Australian Bureau of Statistics, June 2012). The city has a cosmopolitan lifestyle, with thriving arts and hospitality scenes, but beyond the glitz it offers some stunning natural scenery, including serene parks and bushland, the sparkling Swan River and beautiful beaches lining the coast.

▲ *Chinese Dragon Parade in Milligan Street, 1901*

HISTORY OF PERTH

The original inhabitants were the Noongar people, which included a number of sub-groups, who lived in the area for at least 40,000 years prior to European settlement. They called the land on which Perth now sits *Boorloo* and the river *Derbarl Yerrigan*. The river system was a rich source of food and was an integral part of their cultural traditions. The traditional owners have retained their strong connections with the land.

The first Europeans to visit the area were Dutch explorers during the 17th century. More than 200 years later, in 1829, the British claimed possession of the West Coast of New Holland, as it was then known. The British had noted a number of French exploratory voyages and wanted to assert control of the region. In June of that year, Lieutenant Governor James Stirling, who captained the *Parmelia*, established the colony 12 miles (approximately 19 kilometres) from the mouth of the Swan River. Stirling had scouted the area in 1827 and chose the site for its great natural beauty, abundance of fresh water and resources available for building, such as stone, lime and clay. Perth was officially founded on 12 August 1829.

Initially, the colony grew slowly. Much of the land around the Swan River, which was originally thought to be a fertile area for agriculture, proved difficult to cultivate. In the 1840s a decision was made to introduce convicts to accelerate development. The decision was controversial as the colony had been made up of free settlers until that point. Perth was officially proclaimed a city in 1856.

The gold rushes in Coolgardie and Kalgoorlie in the 1890s were a significant factor in Perth's development, as during this period Perth's population trebled. A mineral boom during the 1960s and 1970s and the state's current mining boom have led to further surges in the city's growth.

THE SWAN RIVER

The Swan River, which flows through the heart of Perth, is an iconic feature of the city and indeed the region. It was originally home to an abundance of black swans, which have become a symbol for Western Australia, appearing on the state flag and coat of arms. The river is a popular destination for the city's locals and visitors.

ATTRACTIONS OF PERTH

Some of the main attractions of Perth are the Bell Tower, a set of 18 bells, 12 of which come from St Martin-in-the-Fields, one of London's most famous churches, and Kings Park, a huge inner-city park situated on the shore of the Swan River. Several landmarks are located within the park itself, such as the State War Memorial, DNA Tower, a 15-metre-high spiral-shaped staircase resembling a DNA molecule, and the Western Australian Botanic Garden, which contains a vast collection of flora, including the magnificent wildflowers for which the state is famous. Some highlights of the city's surrounds are nearby Cottesloe Beach, Rottnest Island and Fremantle – which are detailed in the following pages.

▼ *Perth skyline*

Cottesloe Beach

A FAVOURITE SPOT TO RELAX

Situated approximately halfway between Perth's central business district and Fremantle is Cottesloe Beach – a much-loved beach for generations of Western Australians. Since the late 19th century the 1.5-kilometre white-sand beach has been a popular destination among locals for swimming, snorkelling, surfing and relaxing by the sea. In particular, the beach, and its nearby terraced lawns, has become a famous spot for watching the sun sink over the Indian Ocean. Set in from the shore, the suburb of Cottesloe has a bustling hospitality scene with numerous cafes, restaurants and bars.

COTTESLOE'S HISTORY

In 1909 the Cottesloe Surf Life Saving Club was established – this was the first surf lifesaving club in Western Australia and one of the first in the country. The North Cottesloe Surf Life Saving Club was formed just a few years later, in 1912.

A distinctive feature of Cottesloe Beach is the building formerly known as the Indiana Tea House, built in 1910. Initially it was a shack offering refreshments but by the 1920s it had become a lively venue. Today, now simply called Indiana, it is an upmarket restaurant.

In 1936 a concrete pylon was built offshore; it was intended to anchor a shark net but instead became a climbing and diving platform. In recent years, the pylon, sometimes called the bell because of its shape, was redesigned to prevent beachgoers from using it, but it remains another local landmark.

▲ *Cottesloe Beach, 1966*

▶ *The Indiana Tea House*

Rottnest Island

A BEAUTIFUL DESTINATION WITH REMARKABLE WILDLIFE

With a diverse history, 63 beautiful beaches and remarkable wildlife, Rottnest Island is the state's top holiday and daytrip destination. The island was originally part of mainland Australia but became separated around 7000 years ago when the sea level rose. The island is one of a chain of islands near Perth and is composed of limestone, which has influenced its flora and fauna.

One of the main attractions of Rottnest Island is its interesting mix of wildlife – in particular, the native quokka, a marsupial resembling a small kangaroo. Thanks to a lack of predators, the island is one of the few remaining locations where quokkas can be spotted today. Numerous coastal birds can also be seen on Rottnest Island. It has been named a BirdLife International Important Bird Area, as it provides a habitat for breeding populations of species such as fairy terns and banded stilts. The reefs which surround the island are home to an array of coral, fish and crustaceans. A variety of other marine life, such as dolphins, Australian sea lions, New Zealand fur seals and humpback whales, can also be seen in the area.

▲ Crested tern off Rottnest Island

HISTORY OF THE ISLAND

When the first Europeans arrived on the island, it was uninhabited. However, artefacts have since shown the presence of Aboriginal people from at least 6500 years before the sea level rose. The island retains its significance for the local Noongar people, who know it as *Wadjemup*, which means 'place across the water where the spirits go'.

The island was sighted by Dutch explorers throughout the 17th century, although the first Europeans known to have set foot on the island were the crew from the Dutch ship *Waeckende Boeij* in 1658. In 1696, Dutch sailor Willem de Vlamingh named the island *Rottenest*, or 'Rat's Nest', mistaking the quokkas for a large kind of rat. (The 'e' was later dropped to form the name 'Rottnest Island'.)

▲ Quokka

Rottnest Island was settled in the early 1830s, soon after the establishment of the Swan River Colony. The early settlers focused on developing the land for pasture and salt harvesting. However, in 1839, it was decided that the island would become a prison for Aboriginal people. The settlers gave up their land and the prison operated until 1903, but prisoners were forced to work on the island until 1931. Approximately 3700 Aboriginal prisoners were held on Rottnest Island during that period. The conditions were miserable and the treatment of the prisoners was harsh. Tragically, at least 370 prisoners died during that time and were interred in a burial ground on the island. Today, the island retains great cultural significance for the Noongar people but also sad memories of the island's prison years.

From the early 1900s Rottnest Island was developed as a recreation and tourist destination, which it remains today. The island is now a protected A-Class Reserve.

▲ *Rottnest Island*

Fremantle

A DISTINCTIVE PLACE

Fremantle's character is very distinct from Perth's. It is known as a relaxed, environmentally friendly place with a vibrant arts scene and a busy nightlife. It also stands out for its numerous well-preserved Victorian and Georgian buildings, such as the 12-sided Round House, a gaol constructed in 1831 – now the oldest public building in the state. The area has a rich history, encompassing the Whadjuk people's occupation of the land for many thousands of years to its role in the early settlement in Western Australia.

HISTORY OF FREMANTLE

On 2 May 1829 Captain Charles Howe Fremantle, commander of HMS *Challenger*, landed at the south head of the Swan River, raised the British flag and claimed possession of the West Coast of New Holland, as it was then known, on behalf of King George IV. A month later Lieutenant Governor James Stirling arrived to establish the Swan River Colony. Stirling named Fremantle in Captain Charles Fremantle's honour. Stirling made the decision to locate the port at Fremantle and the colony further up the Swan River where there was a plentiful supply of fresh water, natural resources for construction and what was

▲ *Fremantle Harbour, 1973*

◄ *The Round House*

▲ Convict-built section of Fremantle Prison, 1974

thought to be fertile land for farming.

Following a decision in the 1840s to transport convicts to Western Australia, the first 75 arrived in 1850. The convicts were set to work building roads, bridges and other infrastructure, including a new gaol – Fremantle Prison – from limestone quarried at the site. The prison operated from 1855 until 1991. In 2010 Fremantle Prison was named along with ten other Australian convict sites on UNESCO's World Heritage List. There are a number of other examples of convict-built architecture in Fremantle, including the Lunatic Asylum, which is today home to the Fremantle Arts Centre, and the Commissariat, now the Western Australian Museum Shipwreck Galleries.

Until the 1860s the settlement was a whaling centre. A small jetty near Arthur Head was the first port facility. At Bathers Bay, Long Jetty, originally called Ocean Jetty, was constructed in 1873. The jetty played an important role during the 1890s gold rush. Around that same time a project began to develop a functional harbour at Fremantle. One of the main activities included blasting the rocky bar across the Swan River mouth and dredging to deepen the basin. Inner Harbour was opened in 1879, replacing Long Jetty. The city continues to serve as an important working port, operating two harbours.

THE TRADITIONAL OWNERS

The traditional owners of the Fremantle area are the Whadjuk, Noongar people, who call it *Walyalup* and continue to have strong connections with the land. A fascinating oral tradition reflects their deep understanding of the area, particularly the geological changes which occurred over time. This is one of the oldest oral traditions in the world. A significant place for the Whadjuk people is the area around Arthur Head, which they call *Manjaree*. It was used as a gathering place, particularly for trading purposes, and Whadjuk still meet there today.

Margaret River

A TOURIST HOTSPOT

In the south-west corner of the state, approximately 280 kilometres from Perth, lies the town of Margaret River – once a quiet pastoral area but now a tourism hotspot. Its popularity is largely due to a strong reputation in wine production and as a world-renowned surfing location, but it also has stunning natural features, gourmet food and a laid-back lifestyle.

The town of Margaret River is set just in from the coast but is in the heart of the region, usually referred to by the same name, which extends from Cape Naturaliste to Cape Leeuwin and encompasses a number of other attractive towns, such as Busselton, Dunsborough, Yallingup and Augusta.

HISTORY OF THE AREA

The first recorded European sighting of the area was made by the crew of the Dutch ship the *Leeuwin* in 1622. Much later, in 1801, British captain Matthew Flinders named Cape Leeuwin and French explorer Nicolas Baudin named Cape Naturaliste and Geographe Bay. The first European settlers arrived in the region in 1830, following the establishment of King George Sound in 1826 and the Swan River Colony in 1829. Augusta was the first site to be settled and Busselton was developed

◄ *Near Yallingup*

a short time after that, in 1832. The early pioneers found the land near the coast difficult for farming and over time moved inland, where the conditions were more suitable. In the 1850s Alfred Bussell, one of the first settlers in the region, built a homestead known as Ellensbrook, which would become the town site of Margaret River.

THE ATTRACTIONS OF THE REGION

The region boasts pristine beaches with consistent waves and ocean temperature – in other words, excellent surfing conditions. Since the 1970s professional surfing competitions have been held in the area. The annual Telstra Drug Aware Pro surfing event at Surfers Point draws talent from all over Australia and the world. There are also many sheltered coastal locations that are perfect for swimming, snorkelling, fishing, boating and other water sports.

▲ *Cape Leeuwin Lighthouse*

Margaret River developed as a wine region from around 1967. It only produces about three per cent of Australia's wine grapes, but 20 per cent of the nation's premium wines come from the area. Vines cover more than 5000 hectares of the Margaret River region and there are over 200 grape growers and wine producers. Many visitors to the region choose to tour the various wineries, each of which has its own distinct feel.

One of the natural highlights within the region is the Leeuwin-Naturaliste Ridge caves. There are literally hundreds of caves, but just a handful of them are open to visitors. Three of the most popular caves are Lake, Mammoth and Jewel, where fascinating stalactite and stalagmite formations can be seen. Like the cave systems of the Nullarbor Plain area, these caves are intricate karst systems, produced by water dissolving the limestone, and featuring dolines, or sinkholes. Significant archaeological finds have been made within the region's caves, including fossils, animal bones, human remains, stone tools and other artefacts. In particular, Devil's Lair Cave has revealed the presence of Aboriginal people dating back about 48,000 years – it is one of the earliest known sites of human occupation in Australia. Devil's Lair Cave, Ngilgi Cave and other sites have immense cultural and spiritual significance for the South West Boojarah region's traditional owners, collectively known as the Noongar people.

A track that runs from cape to cape – that is, from Cape Leeuwin to Cape Naturaliste – allows walkers to explore the beautiful coastal scenery. At the start of the track is the historic Cape Leeuwin Lighthouse, a striking 39-metre-high building that has helped to guide ships in the area since 1896. The lighthouse is located at the south-westernmost point in Australia, where the Indian and Southern oceans meet.

BUSSELTON JETTY

Another landmark of the area is the Busselton Jetty, which extends 1841 metres into Geographe Bay. The first part of the jetty was completed during the 1860s and it underwent numerous extensions over the years. The Busselton Jetty operated as a working jetty until 1971. An underwater observatory, a recent addition to the site, reveals brightly coloured tropical and subtropical marine plants and animals that live beneath the jetty. It has been described as the greatest artificial reef in the country.

DUNSBOROUGH

The town of Dunsborough is yet another popular destination, particularly during whale watching season, from September to December, when humpback, southern right and pygmy blue whales can be sighted in Geographe Bay. Sunk off the coast of Dunsborough is the former HMAS *Swan* – a naval destroyer that was decommissioned in 1997. It is one of the largest accessible dive wrecks in the Southern Hemisphere.

▼ *Busselton Jetty*

Walpole Wilderness

EXTRAORDINARY OLD-GROWTH FOREST

The Walpole Wilderness Area is an extraordinary part of Western Australia featuring old-growth karri, jarrah and tingle forests as well as coastal heath and wetlands. It is a vast area – some 363,000 hectares in all – and incorporates seven national parks and numerous conservation areas in the state's south-west. The Walpole Wilderness has been described as a 'global biodiversity hotspot' as it is rich in rare plant species and offers habitat for a wide variety of creatures, from big to microscopic. Many of the plant species are endemic to the area – which is to say they are not found anywhere else in the world.

The Walpole Wilderness Area is particularly famous for its towering tingle forests. At the Treetop Walk, also known as the Valley of the Giants, visitors can explore the canopy from a walkway positioned up to 40 metres above the ground then the forest floor from a boardwalk. Another incredible sight is the Giant Tingle Tree – an enormous red tingle with a circumference of 24 metres. The tree has been hollowed out by fire, so visitors can walk inside.

In addition to its important ecological values, the land has great meaning for the traditional owners, the Wagyl Kaip and Southern Noongar people.

▶ *Giant tingle trees*

The Pinnacles

THOUSANDS OF LIMESTONE PILLARS

The Pinnacles Desert – which features thousands of limestone pillars – is one of Australia's most intriguing landscapes. The pillars range in height – some are tiny, while others stand four metres tall. Their shape varies, from rounded to sharp-edged, as does their texture. Most are sandy yellow in colour, but some are pinkish or brown. They are particularly spectacular when seen at dawn or dusk. The Pinnacles capture the imagination of visitors, who often describe the landscape as being eerie and from another planet. Some parts have been likened to a cemetery or even city ruins.

THE FORMATION OF THE PINNACLES

Some aspects of the Pinnacles' formation are unclear, but it is known that the main elements responsible are wind, water and calcium. The sand in the area originated as seashells, which were broken down and carried inland by the wind, making dunes. As vegetation grew among the dunes, a layer of sandy soil, rich in decaying plant matter, developed. When it rained, water seeped through this acidic soil, becoming acidic too. The acidic water dissolved the calcium carbonate in the sand and deposited it in the deeper layers of the soil, binding the particles together and producing limestone. As this process continued, three layers emerged beneath the dunes – vegetation and soil near the surface, a hard cap under that and a soft limestone deep below the surface – and from this the Pinnacles formed. There are differing opinions on exactly how the Pinnacles got their distinctive column shape. Eventually, when the sand dunes shifted, the Pinnacles appeared.

▲ *The Pinnacles Desert*

A STUNNING NATIONAL PARK

The Pinnacles are located within Nambung National Park, approximately 245 kilometres north of Perth. While the Pinnacles are by far the main attraction, the national park offers stunning coastal scenery and a magnificent wildflower display in late winter and spring.

Shark Bay

A PLACE OF OUTSTANDING NATURAL BEAUTY

Located approximately 800 kilometres north of Perth, the World Heritage-listed Shark Bay has a number of very special attributes. The 1500-kilometre stretch of coastline, which is the most westerly point of mainland Australia, offers outstanding natural beauty, with a diverse range of landscapes and seascapes that are home to an array of notable plant and animal life. An unusual feature of the landscape are the birridas, or claypans, which were originally inland saline lakes. Some of these – such as Big Lagoon – have been flooded with sea water, creating stunning turquoise lagoons. In 1991 the area was included on the UNESCO World Heritage List for its rare and important ecological qualities.

HAMELIN POOL

The remote bay is widely known for its unusual and highly significant plant life. In the shallow, hypersaline (extremely concentrated salt) waters of Hamelin Pool, colonies of blue-green algae, or cyanobacteria, have created striking dome-shaped structures, known as stromatolites. These structures have been formed over as many as 3000 years and are among

▼ *Stromatolites, Shark Bay*

the oldest organisms on Earth. They are sometimes described as 'living fossils' because they give insight into the earliest life forms on the planet just like fossils in rocks. The Hamelin Pool stromatolites were a key contributing factor to the area being listed as a UNESCO World Heritage Site.

SIGNIFICANT SEAGRASS MEADOWS

Shark Bay is also the location of extensive seagrass meadows, encompassing over 4800 square kilometres of the bay. The Wooramel Seagrass Bank, which covers an area of more than 1000 square kilometres, is the largest known seagrass bank in the world. An impressive number of plant species are represented in Shark Bay's seagrass meadows, particularly at Wooramel Seagrass Bank. The seagrasses are important ecosystems, providing food and shelter for numerous marine animals, particularly dugong, or sea cows, and turtles.

ABUNDANT MARINE LIFE

The area is famous for its marine animals, including humpback and southern right whales, dugong – approximately one eighth of the world's population of the mammals – as well as bottlenose dolphins, green and loggerhead turtles, sharks, rays and fish. One of the highlights for visitors to the area is the chance of an encounter with wild bottlenose dolphins at Monkey Mia. Since the 1960s dolphins have been coming in to shore to receive a small amount of fish from humans. This rare interaction has become a popular tourist attraction.

DIRK HARTOG ISLAND

Located within Shark Bay is Dirk Hartog Island – the site of the first recorded European landing in Australia. On 25 October 1616 Dutch explorer Captain Dirk Hartog anchored the Dutch East India Company ship, *Eendracht*, and came ashore. He climbed a cliff, which is now known as Cape Inscription, and left his mark on the site by erecting a wooden post and nailing a pewter plate engraved with the details of his voyage into the post. Hartog was followed by a number of other Dutch, French and English explorers in the late 17th and early 18th centuries. Hartog's plate was discovered in 1697 by a Dutch captain, Willem de Vlamingh. It is now kept in the Rijksmuseum in Amsterdam, Holland.

▼ *Cape Inscription Lighthouse, Dirk Hartog Island, c. 1910*

Ningaloo Reef and Cape Range

AN OUTSTANDING MARINE AND COASTAL ENVIRONMENT

On the mid north coast, approximately 1200 kilometres from Perth, is Ningaloo Reef and Cape Range – an outstanding marine and coastal environment, which was UNESCO World Heritage listed in 2011. The 6000-square-kilometre site was recognised for its immense natural beauty, high biological diversity and conservation importance.

NINGALOO REEF

Ningaloo Reef stretches 260 kilometres southwards from the Exmouth Gulf to Red Bluff. It is the country's largest fringing coral reef. It is also unusual for a coral reef to be located so close to the shore. In fact, Ningaloo Reef is one of the world's longest near-shore reefs.

The reef supports an abundance of life, including more than 200 species of coral and over 500 species of fish. Many of these are spectacular, such as the whale shark, which is the largest species of fish, and some are endangered, such as the loggerhead sea turtles. Other notable marine life that visits

▶ *Whale shark, Ningaloo Reef*

the area includes humpback whales, dugong, dolphins and manta rays. Not surprisingly, Ningaloo Marine Park has become a popular spot for snorkelling, scuba diving and boating.

▲ *Green sea turtle, Ningaloo Reef*

CAPE RANGE

Beyond the reef, the adjoining coastline is remarkable in its own right. Within the Cape Range region, there are many intriguing limestone formations, including sinkholes and cave systems, plummeting gorges, such as the stunning multi-coloured rock walls surrounding Yardie Creek, and unspoiled beaches. It also holds a treasure trove of fossilised marine creatures up to millions of years old. At Mandu Mandu Rock Shelter, archaeologists have noted the earliest evidence of the use of fish and shellfish by Aboriginal people, dating more than 30,000 years ago.

The Gnulli people have been recognised as the traditional owners of the land.

▼ *Cape Range*

The Kimberley

A VAST AREA WITH INCREDIBLE SCENERY

The Kimberley is a truly inspiring vast region in northern Western Australia. It covers 423,517 square kilometres, representing one sixth of the state – and is twice the size of Victoria. The rugged natural landscape varies from dramatic mountain ranges with spectacular gorges, waterfalls and cave systems to spinifex plains, and undergoes enormous transformation through the seasons. There are two distinct seasons, with tropical rain and storms during the wet season from November to April and clear, sunny days during the dry season from May to October. The wet season, which brings 90 per cent of the region's rainfall, results in the flooding of many of the rivers, such as the Fitzroy River. The Kimberley has a rich Aboriginal heritage, with a number of groups living in the region from as long as 40,000 years ago. Approximately half of the Kimberley's population is Aboriginal, with 30 language groups represented.

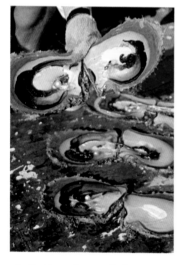

▲ *Cultured pearls from Kuri Bay and Broome*

BROOME

Originally a pearling port, Broome is the largest town in the region and the gateway to the Kimberley. The pearling industry thrived during the 19th century and the town of Broome, named after the Governor of Western Australia, Sir Frederick Broome, was proclaimed in 1883. At its peak, the area provided up to 80 per cent of the world's pearl shell output. World War I had a devastating impact on the industry, with men enlisting to serve their country and the product no longer in demand across the world. Following the war, the town and industry gained momentum but were crippled by the outbreak of World War II. Once more, however, they recovered. During the late 1950s Broome's pearling industry found new life with an emerging market in cultured pearls. Pearling is still one of the major industries in the Kimberley and Broome has the reputation of producing some of the finest pearls in the world.

Today, tourism plays an important role in the local economy. The city's permanent population is approximately 15,000 but in peak season this number can treble. Visitors to Broome can explore Chinatown – with the Chinese being just one of the nationalities drawn to the area in the hope of finding their fortune – the historic Streeter's Jetty, originally used by the pearling luggers, and, a short distance outside of the town, at Willie Creek Pearl Farm, learn how cultured pearls are produced.

Each year from March to October a wonderful natural phenomenon occurs along the coastline in the area. Known as Staircase to the Moon, the light of the full moon reflecting off the exposed mudflats of Roebuck Bay at very low tide creates the impression of stairs leading to the moon.

CABLE BEACH

A famous landmark of the area is Cable Beach – a beautiful 22-kilometre stretch of white sand and turquoise water six kilometres from Broome. The beach got its name from the historic telegraph cable that was laid between Broome and Java in 1889, linking Australia's north-west with the world. Camel rides along the beach at sunset are a popular activity.

▲ *Dinosaur footprints at Gantheaume Point*

A fascinating nearby attraction is Gantheaume Point, where the footprints of dinosaurs, believed to be 130 million years old, preserved in the reef rock, can be seen at low tide.

DERBY

Approximately 230 kilometres north-east of Broome, at King Sound, Derby is one of only three towns in the region with a population greater than 3000. Derby is famous for its boab trees, notably the Boab Prison Tree on the outskirts of the town – a hollow boab, thought to be around 1500 years old, measuring more than 14 metres in circumference.

One of the main local attractions, in the Buccaneer Archipelago, is the Horizontal Falls – yet another incredible natural phenomenon of the Kimberley. Despite the name, these are actually powerful tidal movements between two narrow gaps in Talbot Bay that create the effect of a 'horizontal' waterfall. Sir David Attenborough has described the falls as one of the world's greatest natural wonders. The Buccaneer Archipelago is magnificent in its own right, dotted with more than 800 islands, with rainforest, mangroves and sandy beaches. On some of the islands and

▲ *Geikie Gorge
National Park*

nearby mainland, rock art is found, reflecting a long Aboriginal history in the area.

FITZROY CROSSING

Fitzroy Crossing, approximately 390 kilometres east of Broome, is a small town on the banks of the Fitzroy River. The area was settled by Europeans during the 1880s but Aboriginal people have lived in the area for many thousands of years. It is now a popular destination for travellers through the Kimberley region, with Geikie Gorge National Park, situated 18 kilometres from the town, being the main attraction. Geikie Gorge is part of a 350-million-year-old limestone barrier reef that stretches across the West Kimberley. Water levels in the gorge, which was carved out by the powerful Fitzroy River, vary dramatically between the dry and wet season. The gorge has towering multi-coloured walls, stained orange, yellow and grey by the fluctuating water levels – a magnificent sight. The gorge is surrounded by plant and bird life, and the waters are teeming with fish, including sawfish and stingrays; freshwater crocodiles are also plentiful. The traditional owners of this land are the Bunaba people, who call the gorge *Darngku*.

HALLS CREEK

Halls Creek, situated about 290 kilometres east of Fitzroy Crossing, was the location of the state's first gold discovery, in 1885, which led to thousands of prospectors flocking to the area. Remnants of the gold rush days can be seen at the original town site, called Old Halls Creek. One of the main local attractions is China Wall, a natural quartz formation that rises up to six metres high, which bears some resemblance to the Great Wall of China, hence its name. Today, Halls Creek is primarily an agricultural and mining service centre but also a gateway for tourists to regional highlights, such as Wolfe Creek Crater National Park and Purnululu National Park.

WOLFE CREEK CRATER

Approximately 150 kilometres south of Halls Creek, on the edge of the Great Sandy Desert, is the Wolfe Creek Crater, within the national park of the same name. It is an enormous crater, more than 800 metres across and with the floor about 60 metres below the rim, created when a meteorite crashed to Earth thousands of years ago. The local Aboriginal people, the Djaru, call the crater *Kandimalal* and its appearance is explained in their Dreamtime story.

PURNULULU NATIONAL PARK

North-east of Halls Creek is the remarkable Bungle Bungle Range, or *Purnululu* as the traditional owners know it. The range has a most unusual appearance with enormous sandstone domes, which have been eroded over 20 million years. The domes, which have orange, grey and black horizontal bands and rise more than 250 metres, have been likened to giant beehives. Between the domes there is a network of deep gorges. In some parts lush vegetation, such as fan palms, appears – an unusual sight in this part of the country. In 1987 Purnululu National Park and Purnululu Conservation Reserve were established. The remote area's great natural beauty and geological significance were officially recognised in 2003 when it was inscribed on UNESCO's World Heritage List. The park is jointly managed by the Department of Conservation and Land Management and the two Aboriginal groups with connections to the area, the Kija and the Djaru, for whom it has strong cultural and spiritual significance.

▲ *Cathedral Gorge*

KUNUNURRA

In the far north-east of the Kimberley, just a short distance from the border with the Northern Territory, is the town of Kununurra. The remote town is more than 1000 kilometres from any major city: over 3000 kilometres from Perth and over 1000 kilometres from Darwin. The landscape surrounding the town is stunning, with many rivers, waterfalls, ranges and gorges to explore. Some of the local sights include Mirima National Park and the Ord River Irrigation Area, with Lake Argyle and Lake Kununurra being the focal points. At Mirima National Park, also known as 'Hidden Valley', similar smaller rock formations to those found in Purnululu National Park can be seen. For this reason this picturesque location is sometimes called a 'Mini Bungle Bungle'. The park gets its name from the traditional owners, the Miriuwung and Gajerrong people, who call the area *Mirima* and for whom the land has great cultural and spiritual value. Lake Argyle is Australia's largest man-made reservoir and is now a thriving ecosystem. The Lake Argyle and Kununurra wetlands support a wide variety of significant animal life, a fact which has been recognised by their listing as a Ramsar (Wetlands of International Importance) site. South of Kununurra is the Argyle Diamond Mine, which is one of the largest diamond-producing mines in the world and the primary source of rare beautiful pink diamonds.

GIBB RIVER ROAD

Stretching from the Wyndham and Kununurra junction of the Great Northern Highway approximately 660 kilometres west to Derby is the Gibb River Road. The route, originally a cattle road, is popular with travellers as it provides access to some incredible scenery with ranges, gorges, rock pools and waterfalls, diverse plant and animal life and the chance to learn about the area's rich Aboriginal heritage. Within the area are the breathtaking Mitchell Falls on the Mitchell Plateau.

◄ *Mitchell Falls*

EACH YEAR A SWIMMING EVENT IS HELD BETWEEN COTTESLOE BEACH AND NEARBY ROTTNEST ISLAND – IT IS ONE OF THE LARGEST OPEN WATER RACES IN THE WORLD.

Close to 10,000 convicts were sent to the Swan River Colony between 1850 and 1868, when transportation ended.

In 2004 the Swan River was named Western Australia's first official heritage icon on the 175th anniversary of the Swan River Colony.

ALTHOUGH THE PINNACLES ARE NOW A MAJOR TOURIST DESTINATION, THEY WERE LARGELY UNHEARD OF UNTIL THE 1960s.

The giant tingle tree in the Walpole Wilderness Area is thought to be the largest girthed living eucalypt in the world.

'This is devil's country;
he's even emptied his bag
of marbles around the place!'

John Ross, on the Devils Marbles

NORTHERN TERRITORY

ARAFURA SEA

WI ISLANDS
MELVILLE ISLAND
Pirlangimpi
Milikapiti
Nguiu

Cape Croker
Croker Island
Minjilang
Mount
COBOURG
PENINSULA

Marchinb
Isl

VAN DIEMEN GUL

CLARENCE STRAIT

Chambers
Bay
Fin

DARWIN
Palmerston
Belyuen
Howard Springs
Point Stuart
Humpty Doo
Mt Bundey
181

DUNDAS STRAIT

Batchelor

Adelaide Ri

Hayes Creek
Emerald Springs
Tipperary
Pine

Greenwood
Nauiyu
(Daly River)

Daly

River

ppimenarti
eats)
arriyanga

Dorisvale

Wombungi
River
aurice

Scott Creek

200

MBARRAN RA

RIVER
Willeroo
Victoria River
Delamere

vergne
Timber Creek

STOKES R

Bullita Outstation
Victoria River Downs

Yarralin

Top Springs

River

Mount Sanford

Victoria

River

Daguragu
Kalkarindji

Mt Farquharson
444

a Lake

Lajamanu

Lake Buck
TANAMI DESERT

Rabbit Flat

Mt Davidson

NORTHERN

Hidden V

Dunmar

Murranji

Newcastle Ck

Beetaloo

Newcastle Waters

Elliott

Lake
Woods

200

Powell Creek

Renner Springs

Warrego

Mt Samuel
430

McLaren Creek

Ucharonidge

Eva Downs

Tarrabool Lake

Banka Banka

Brunchilly

Rockhampton Downs

Alroy Downs

Three Ways
Tennant Creek

TERRITORY

McArthur River

Mallapunyah
Springs

Robinson

BARKLY

Anthony
Lagoon

Cresswell

Cresswell Downs

Creek

Brunette Downs
Corella Lake

De Burgh Lake

Barkly

Robins

Calvert Hills

Benmara

Mt Drum
Mittie

Sylvester Lake

Alexandria

Ranken

Ranken

Soudan

Wenny
Se

River

S

Darwin

A VIBRANT, HISTORIC CITY

Darwin has the smallest population of all Australian capital cities, with just 127,532 people (Australian Bureau of Statistics, 2013). Despite this, Darwin is a vibrant city with many cultural influences. It serves as the Northern Territory's main commercial and administrative hub and an entrance to the area's spectacular locations, such as the World Heritage-listed sites of Kakadu National Park and Uluru-Kata Tjuta National Park, which have become icons of Australia. The city is often described as Australia's gateway to South-East Asia for business and industry, particularly livestock exports, given its geographical proximity to the region. It is a very modern city, with the unfortunate distinction of having been rebuilt twice – first due to the Japanese air raids in 1942 and 1943 and again following the devastation caused by Tropical Cyclone Tracy in 1974.

▲ *Darwin skyline*

THE HISTORY OF THE AREA

The original inhabitants of the Darwin area were the Larrakia people, also known as the Gulumirrgin. The Larrakia still live in the vicinity and are prominent members of the community.

The first Europeans to visit the region were Dutch explorers during the 17th century. It was the Dutch who first mapped the area, giving Dutch names to a number of places including Arnhem Land and Groote Eylandt. Port Darwin was first discovered by British explorers in 1839 when HMS *Beagle*, captained by John Clements Wickham, sailed into the harbour. Wickham named the port after the naturalist Charles Darwin who had travelled with them on an earlier expedition.

Initial attempts to settle the area failed. Then, the Surveyor General of South Australia, G.W. Goyder, was sent to establish a settlement. Goyder arrived on 5 February 1869 with a party of 135 and immediately began work on the layout. He called the settlement Palmerston after the British Prime Minister Lord Palmerston. This was later changed to Darwin in 1911.

The town grew rapidly after the discovery of gold at Pine Creek, approximately 200 kilometres south, during the

▲ *Wood engraving of the planting of the first pole on the Overland Telegraph Line to Carpentaria by Samuel Calvert, c. 1870*

installation of telegraph poles for the Overland Telegraph Line. From the 1880s the development of the pearling industry led to further expansion of the town, attracting people from Europe, Asia and the South Sea Islands. Darwin was granted the status of city in 1956.

THE BOMBING OF DARWIN

During World War II, Darwin played a crucial role in Australia's defence. Following the outbreak of war in the Pacific, the military presence in Darwin was quickly bolstered. The city served as a major base from which to deploy troops, aircraft and ships to the north. On 19 February 1942 the city and harbour were bombed extensively by Japanese aircraft. In that attack, which included two air raids on the same day, eight ships were sunk, numerous buildings were damaged or destroyed, essential services were disrupted and at least 250 people were killed. These were the first and most serious attacks mounted by a foreign power on Australia. They were followed by many attacks on Darwin, with 64 air raids between February 1942 and November 1943.

▲ *The ruins of the post office after the first Japanese raid, Darwin, 1942*

TROPICAL CYCLONE TRACY

Unfortunately, just over 30 years later, Darwin would be hit by an even more destructive force – this time, of the natural kind. In the early hours of Christmas Day, Tropical Cyclone Tracy passed directly over Darwin, devastating the city and killing 65 people – 49 in the city and a further 16 at sea – and injuring many more. As a result of one of Australia's worst natural disasters, most of the city's buildings were completely destroyed or severely compromised and all public services were cut. A huge emergency response began and the vast majority of the city's inhabitants were evacuated, many of whom chose never to return. In the years that followed Darwin was rebuilt, this time with greater provision for the threat of natural disasters. The damage bill was in the hundreds of millions of dollars. It was one of the most significant tropical cyclones in Australia's history.

DARWIN TODAY

Today, Darwin is one of Australia's most multicultural places – people of around 60 different nationalities live there. Its diversity can be traced back to the settlement's days as a pearling port and of course to its proximity to South-East Asia. Darwin's multicultural influences are evident at the various cultural events held throughout the year and in the eclectic variety of food and dining options.

ATTRACTIONS OF DARWIN

▲ *Crocodile, Northern Territory*

Darwin is famous for its laid-back, tropical lifestyle. It is an attractive city with many expansive streets and abundant lush vegetation – perhaps best experienced at the George Brown Darwin Botanic Gardens. Outdoor dining is very popular, particularly at the recently developed Darwin Waterfront Precinct. Darwin also has a bustling market scene. In fact, the city's main tourist attraction is the Mindil Beach Sunset Markets, with hundreds of stalls offering cuisines and arts and crafts from all over the world. Lake Alexander at East Point Reserve provides a safe spot for swimming year round and is also a great place for picnics, barbecues, walking and cycling. Swimming at the beaches around Darwin is not recommended due to the threats of box jellyfish and crocodiles, especially during the wet season.

▲ *Mindil Beach*

Darwin's rich history can be explored in a variety of ways. Lyons Cottage – the former British–Australian Telegraph's headquarters for the Australian Overland Telegraph – is one of the city's oldest surviving buildings and provides insights into the early days of the settlement. The Australian Pearling Exhibition traces the history of pearling in the region. The Defence of Darwin Experience is an exciting exhibition space housed in a new building within the Darwin Military Museum Precinct at East Point. In just a short time since opening in 2012, the interactive exhibition has become one of Darwin's major visitor attractions. The Museum and Art Gallery of the Northern Territory showcases the region's art, history and culture, and natural history. A significant event on the museum's calendar is the annual Telstra National Aboriginal and Torres Strait Islander Art Award.

Kakadu National Park

A VERY SPECIAL PLACE

Approximately 240 kilometres east of Darwin is Kakadu National Park, a place of extraordinary natural beauty and diversity and with a thriving culture that dates back tens of thousands of years. Kakadu National Park is Australia's largest terrestrial (land-based) national park, encompassing a vast area of nearly 20,000 square kilometres. It was established in three stages between 1979 and 1991. The park's qualities are considered to be so special that it gained a prestigious UNESCO World Heritage listing in 1981 acknowledging its superb natural and cultural features. The inclusion area has been extended several times since then.

Many different ecosystems are represented within the park. At the northern end are mangroves, changing to monsoon rainforest, billabongs and open woodland as one journeys further south. Kakadu is home to a wide range of flora and fauna. Many of these are rare or endemic – which means they are unique to the area. Notably, there are approximately 2000 species of plants. Billabongs abundant with waterlilies have become one of the iconic images of Kakadu. The national park supports more than one third of Australia's bird species – about 280 kinds – and one quarter of its freshwater and estuarine fish. Kakadu's wetlands, which include a variety of types, have been listed under the Ramsar Convention on Wetlands of International Importance.

▲ *Great white egret*

THE TRADITIONAL OWNERS

Kakadu's traditional owners are from a number of different clan groups that speak different languages. Known as the Bininj/Mungguy people, they have occupied this land for up to 50,000 years. *Bininj* is a Kun-winjku and Gun-djeihmi word, reflecting the languages of the north-eastern and central parts respectively, while *Mungguy* is a Jawoyn word reflecting

▲ *Water lilies*

▲ *Aboriginal rock art*

▲ *Jim Jim Falls*

the language of the southern part. The Bininj/Mungguy people own about half the land in Kakadu and lease it as a national park, allowing this outstanding country to be shared and the traditional owners to gain income and employment opportunities. The traditional owners manage the park together with Parks Australia. The name 'Kakadu' comes from one of the languages previously spoken in the north called *Gagudgu*.

Rock paintings, carvings and archaeological sites are found throughout Kakadu. There are more than 5000 rock art sites within the park, some of which are sacred. The rock art of Kakadu provides one of the longest historical records of any people in the world. Some of the rock paintings depict scenes from early contact with Europeans. Two of the main art sites are the rock shelters at Nourlangie and Ubirr.

HIGHLIGHTS OF KAKADU

Kakadu's focal points are the East Alligator region, including Ubirr and the Manngarre Rainforest; the South Alligator region, including the Mamukala Wetlands; the Nourlangie region, with Nourlangie and Nanguluwur rock art sites and Anbangbang Billabong, one of the park's most attractive billabongs; the Yellow Water Wetland area and the spectacular Jim Jim Falls – over which water cascades more than 200 metres – and Twin Falls.

ARNHEM LAND

To the east of Kakadu, in the isolated north-east corner of the Northern Territory, is Arnhem Land. The area, which covers roughly 97,000 square kilometres, offers unspoiled, contrasting scenery, a fascinating cultural heritage and plenty of wildlife. Situated on the Arnhem Land Plateau, the landscape consists of stunning coastline, islands, rivers, rainforests, escarpments and woodlands. It provides the habitat for crocodiles, dugong and migratory birds, among many other creatures.

Access to Arnhem Land is restricted – only approved tour operators can bring visitors to the area – making it one of the least visited places in Australia. Arnhem Land is said to be the place where the didjeridu originated. But more importantly, it provides the opportunity to experience the continuing traditions of the Yolngu people, in the north-east, who have maintained their traditional culture.

Nitmiluk Gorge

KEY FACT
A NAME CHANGE
FOR A FAMOUS
LANDMARK

A BREATHTAKING GORGE SYSTEM

Nitmiluk Gorge, a deep gorge that has been etched out of sandstone and conglomerate by the Katherine River, is a breathtaking natural feature of Nitmiluk National Park. The gorge system, which consists of 13 gorges, stretches approximately 13 kilometres. The mostly sheer surrounding walls reach higher than 70 metres. It is a place of great natural beauty and tremendous cultural and historical value.

Nitmiluk National Park, encompassing an area of more than 2900 square kilometres, is located 244 kilometres south-east of Darwin. The gorge and the park were previously known as Katherine Gorge and Katherine Gorge National Park respectively, but the names were changed when the land was handed back to the traditional owners, the Jawoyn people.

THE TRADITIONAL OWNERS

The park has enormous significance for the Jawoyn people, who have maintained their connections with the land. Today, they jointly manage the park together with the Parks and Wildlife Commission of the Northern Territory. The name 'Nitmiluk' comes from a story about the creation being Nabilil, who named the entrance to the gorge after the sound of cicadas.

Rock art is found on sandstone walls throughout the park, reflecting the presence of the Jawoyn people for many thousands of years. In fact, there are more than 400 art sites in the park with further examples still being uncovered.

◀ *Nitmiluk Gorge*

There are numerous sites in Nitmiluk National Park that are significant to the Jawoyn people, some of which are sensitive or sacred locations.

A walking trail within the park, called Jatbula Trail, traces the journey made by generations of Jawoyn people between the gorge and Leliyn (Edith Falls) on the western side of the park. The trail, which extends approximately 60 kilometres, is named after Peter Jatbula who played a vital role in the negotiations between the Jawoyn people and the government for the return of Nitmiluk to the traditional owners. Leliyn is a popular swimming spot.

A DIVERSE LANDSCAPE

There is a diverse range of ecosystems within Nitmiluk National Park, including sandstone plateau heath, riverine habitats, woodlands, open forest and rainforest patches in moist gullies. An impressive 750 plant species have been recorded within the park. The fauna consists of 206 bird species, 78 reptile species, 44 native mammal species and 39 fish species, to name just a few groups. Freshwater crocodiles, which are generally considered harmless, live in the river throughout the year. Estuarine, or saltwater, crocodiles, which pose a threat to human life, can appear during the wet season when water levels rise. At this time of year swimming and canoeing are prohibited. Crocodile management is one of a number of responsibilities of the park's managers.

The northern side of Nitmiluk National Park borders Kakadu National Park, one of Australia's most famous landscapes.

▶ *Nitmiluk Gorge*

Devils Marbles

KEY FACT
GREAT
NATURAL
WONDER

A SYMBOL OF AUSTRALIA'S OUTBACK

The Devils Marbles – a collection of ancient smooth granite boulders, some of which balance delicately on top of each other – are one of Australia's great natural wonders. The boulders vary in size, from 50 centimetres to six metres in diameter, and appear to have been scattered across the wide, open valley. Located within Devils Marbles Conservation Reserve, they have become a familiar symbol of Australia's Outback.

The Devils Marbles reportedly got their name from John Ross, who, when leading a survey for the Overland Telegraph in 1870, commented: 'This is devil's country; he's even emptied his bag of marbles around the place!' To the Aboriginal groups who have inhabited this country for thousands of years – the Warumungu, Kaytetye, Alyawarra and Warlpiri people – the boulders are known as *Karlu Karlu* (which means 'round boulders').

THE FORMATION OF THE 'MARBLES'

The 'marbles' were formed when magma, from deep within the Earth, cooled, producing a solid mass of granite. Originally, the granite sat beneath a sandstone layer, but this was broken down and eventually the granite was revealed. The granite cracked and split into both vertical and horizontal blocks. Over millions of years, those blocks were shaped by spheroidal weathering – a process which still continues – into the smooth rounded boulders that are seen today.

▲ *Devils Marbles*

A SACRED SITE

The site is extremely sacred – in fact, the majority of the conservation reserve is protected under the Northern Territory Aboriginal Sacred Sites Act. In 2008 the land was returned to the traditional owners. The reserve is now leased to the Parks and Wildlife Commission of the Northern Territory and is jointly managed by the commission and the traditional owners.

Approximately 100 kilometres to the south is Tennant Creek, the location of Australia's last gold rush, in 1932.

Alice Springs

A FAMOUS OUTBACK LOCATION

The remote town of Alice Springs is one of Australia's most famous Outback locations. It lies near the southern border of the Northern Territory and is almost equidistant from the two closest capital cities, Darwin and Adelaide. It is the third largest settlement in the Northern Territory after Darwin and Palmerston respectively. Of all Australian towns, it is the furthest from the coast. The town is the service centre for the region and a gateway to the numerous tourist attractions of the Red Centre, such as the MacDonnell Ranges, Watarrka National Park, Uluru-Kata Tjuta National Park and the Simpson Desert.

THE HISTORY OF THE AREA

The original inhabitants are the Arrernte people, who have occupied the area for many thousands of years. The Arrernte people call Alice Springs *Mparntwe* and have maintained their culture and connections with the land.

In 1862 the explorer John McDouall Stuart was the first European to visit the region, passing near to what would later become the town site of Alice Springs. In 1871, during the construction of the Overland Telegraph Line, a surveyor called William Whitfield Mills discovered what he thought to be a permanent water source in the area. Mills named the main waterhole 'Alice Spring' after Alice Todd, who was the wife of the South Australian Superintendent of Telegraphs, Sir Charles Todd. The Alice Springs Telegraph Station was

▶ *Alice Springs*

built near the waterhole. The Todd River, which is usually dry, was named in Sir Charles's honour. Soon thereafter pastoralists began taking up leases in the area. It was the discovery of alluvial gold in the region in 1887 which truly accelerated the growth of the settlement. The town was called Stuart until 1933 when it was changed to Alice Springs.

In 1929 the railway line connecting Alice Springs with Adelaide was completed and was finally extended through to Darwin in 2004. The resulting transcontinental railway line, called *The Ghan*, is one of Australia's most well-known railway journeys.

ALICE SPRINGS'S ATTRACTIONS

Anzac Hill, a war memorial that offers fantastic views of the town and the nearby MacDonnell Ranges, is Alice Springs's most popular landmark. Visitors can discover the area's rich Aboriginal heritage in the Araluen Cultural Precinct and at Alice Springs Desert Park, which has local Aboriginal guides. Numerous sites provide insight into how the settlement developed from those early pioneering times into the town it is today: the Telegraph Station Historical Reserve; Old Stuart Town Gaol; Hartley Street School; Adelaide House, the region's first hospital; The Residency, the historic home of the Government Resident of Central Australia; and the Royal Flying Doctor Service Base, to name just a handful.

Several quirky annual events are held in Alice Springs, such as the Henley-on-Todd Regatta, a 'waterless regatta' in which boats are carried along the dry bed of the Todd River. The fun event, which raises money for charity, has been running for more than 50 years.

HERMANNSBURG

Hermannsburg, approximately 140 kilometres from Alice Springs, was established in 1877 as a German Lutheran mission for Aboriginal people. The mission served as a refuge for Arrernte people at a time of upheaval and violent conflict with the European settlers. The famous Aboriginal artist, Albert Namatjira, was born and grew up in Hermannsburg. Today, visitors can explore this historic precinct, including the old mission house and Albert Namatjira's home. In 1982 the land was returned to its traditional owners.

▲ *Henley-on-Todd Regatta, 1999*

▼ *Portrait of Albert Namatjira at Hermannsburg Mission, 1946 or 1947*

Kings Canyon

AN AWE-INSPIRING LANDSCAPE

Located almost halfway between Alice Springs and Uluṟu, at the western end of the George Gill Range, is Kings Canyon, an awe-inspiring landscape. The canyon's sheer sandstone walls rise from Kings Creek up to 270 metres. On the plateau above, there are many striking dome-shaped rock formations, similar to some of those in the World Heritage-listed Purnululu National Park in Western Australia. In sheltered gullies, lush vegetation grows, in stark contrast to the surrounding dry country.

▲▼ Kings Canyon from above

WATARRKA NATIONAL PARK

The canyon is part of Watarrka National Park and is one of the Northern Territory's major tourist attractions, with approximately 215,000 visitors each year. There are several walking tracks within the area. The Kings Creek Walk allows visitors to explore the bottom of the gorge and the base of the towering canyon walls. The Canyon Walk offers vertigo-producing views of the gorge below, a waterhole known as the Garden of Eden where plant life abounds, and the fascinating striped sandstone domes along the canyon rim. The Giles Track is a more challenging walk connecting Kings Canyon with Kathleen Springs.

Watarrka National Park was formally declared a park in 1989. It is an important conservation area, providing refuge to hundreds of plant and animal species, including some which are rare and threatened.

It also has a rich cultural heritage. The Luritja people have lived in the area for many thousands of years and there are a number of important cultural and spiritual sites within the park. In an agreement made in 2012 the Luritja people were granted title over more than 1000 square kilometres within Watarrka National Park.

Uluṟu and Kata Tjuṯa

TWO MAJOR POINTS OF INTEREST

Each year hundreds of thousands of visitors make the journey to the World Heritage-listed Uluṟu-Kata Tjuṯa National Park in the heart of Australia's Red Centre. There are two major points of interest within the park: Uluṟu, also known as Ayers Rock, and Kata Tjuṯa, also known as Mount Olga or simply The Olgas. Uluṟu is a magnificent rock formation that reaches 348 metres above the surrounding plain (860 metres above sea level) and has a circumference of 9.4 kilometres. It has smooth sloped sides and a mostly flat top. It has become an icon of the arid Central Australian landscape. Approximately 30 kilometres west of Uluṟu is Kata Tjuṯa, a group of large, intriguing rock domes – 36 in all. Its highest point is 546 metres above the plain (1066 metres above sea level). Uluṟu and Kata Tjuṯa are thought to have been formed about 500 million years ago. Both features have a distinctive orange-red colour.

▼ *Uluṟu*

▲ *Kata Tjuṯa*

ULUṞU-KATA TJUṮA NATIONAL PARK

Situated approximately 450 kilometres south-west of Alice Springs by road, Uluṟu-Kata Tjuṯa National Park covers an area of 1325 square kilometres. Ayers Rock, as it was called then, was declared a national park in 1950. Eight years later Mount Olga was included in the park area. In addition to Uluṟu and Kata Tjuṯa, the landscape includes sand dunes, plains and desert, with vegetation ranging from spinifex grasses to shrubs and trees, some of which are rare or unique to the area. Among the fauna, 21 native mammals and 150 bird species are found.

KATA TJUṮA

The first European to sight Kata Tjuṯa was explorer Ernest Giles in 1872. At the request of his benefactor Baron Ferdinand von Mueller, Giles named it 'Mount Olga', in honour of Queen Olga of Württemberg, who had granted Mueller his title. The first European to sight Uluṟu was explorer William Gosse the following year. Gosse named it 'Ayers Rock' after the Chief Secretary of South Australia at that time, Sir Henry Ayers.

THE TRADITIONAL OWNERS

The Anangu people are the traditional owners of Uluṟu and Kata Tjuṯa. They have lived in the region for tens of thousands of years. There are many examples of rock paintings in Uluṟu-Kata Tjuṯa National Park, which reflect the Anangu's long connection with the area. Guided by the traditional law of

Tjukurpa, they continue to practise their cultural traditions today. The landscapes within the park hold immense meaning for the Anangu people.

The Anangu campaigned for more than 35 years for their traditional ownership to be recognised. On 26 October 1985 they were finally handed back their land. The Anangu celebrate the anniversary of this handback each year. The land is leased to Parks Australia, who manage the land together with the Anangu. In 1993 dual names for the two features, Ayers Rock/Uluru and Mount Olga/Kata Tjuta, were made official and in 2002 the order of those dual names was changed to Uluru/Ayers Rock and Kata Tjuta/Mount Olga out of respect for the traditional owners. Anangu people prefer that tourists do not climb Uluru, which has enormous meaning for them; instead, there are a variety of walks visitors can do to experience Uluru and discover Anangu culture.

A WORLD HERITAGE AREA

In 1987 Uluru-Kata Tjuta National Park was named a UNESCO World Heritage Area for its globally significant natural attributes. In 1994 it gained World Heritage listing as a universally important cultural landscape. The following year the park was awarded the Picasso Gold Medal, which is the highest UNESCO award for outstanding efforts to preserve both the environment and Anangu culture and for raising the bar for World Heritage management.

▲ *Uluru-Kata Tjuta National Park Handover/ Leaseback Ceremony, 1985*

Darwin is closer to Jakarta, the capital of Indonesia, than it is to Canberra, Australia's national capital.

Kakadu National Park is croc central – with a population of more than 10,000 crocodiles!

Alice Springs's Henley-on-Todd Regatta had to be cancelled in 1994 because there was too much water in the Todd River!

Alice Springs is commonly called 'the Alice' or simply 'Alice'.

'My father says there has been a forest here for over a hundred million years [...]'

Jeannie Baker, *Where the Forest Meets the Sea*, set in the Daintree Rainforest

QUEENSLAND

Brisbane

A THRIVING CAPITAL CITY

Brisbane is the capital and the largest city in Queensland. With a population of more than 2 million people, it is the third largest city in Australia and has a thriving economy. It is an important hub for business, with most major Australian companies and many international ones choosing to have a presence there. The city is situated on the Brisbane River, which snakes 27 kilometres from the central business district to the river's mouth at Moreton Bay. Brisbane stands out as an attractive city with a relaxed, appealing, outdoor lifestyle.

▲ *Brisbane skyline*

THE HISTORY OF THE CITY

The traditional owners of the area were the Turrbal people, who primarily lived north of the river, and the Jagera, who lived south of the river. Brisbane's Indigenous name is *Mian-jin* which means 'place shaped like a spike'.

The first European visitor was Matthew Flinders, who explored Moreton Bay in 1799. In 1823 the Governor of New South Wales, Sir Thomas Brisbane, decided that a northern penal colony should be established. A party, led by Surveyor General John Oxley, was sent from Sydney to determine a suitable location for the colony within the region. In 1824 a settlement was established at Redcliffe Point by Lieutenant Henry Miller. The following year, the settlement was moved from Redcliffe to its present site on the Brisbane River, which offered a better freshwater supply. From 1838 it was opened to free settlers. The Municipality of Brisbane was proclaimed in 1859.

AN INTERESTING ARCHITECTURAL MIX

Today, the city has an interesting mix of modern architecture, including skyscrapers, and heritage buildings. Some of Brisbane's noteworthy historic buildings include the Commissariat Stores, which was built by convicts in 1829; Customs House, built in 1889; Parliament House, built in 1868; and Brisbane City Hall, built between 1920 and 1930 and opened in 1930.

Brisbane City Hall is a magnificent sandstone building with a 92-metre-high clock tower and grand Corinthian columns at its entrance. The newly restored city hall is one of the state's principal heritage landmarks and hosts many important cultural, social and civic functions. The city hall is located in King George Square, an open-air public space used for markets, games nights and other community events.

A DESIRABLE OUTDOOR LIFESTYLE

Brisbane's pleasant subtropical climate promotes a desirable lifestyle that is centred on riverside and al fresco dining, shopping and entertainment. A favourite outdoor activity for locals and visitors is RiverWalk, a network of pathways, roads, bridges and parks that runs for more than 20 kilometres alongside the river. The city also has a range of open-air markets, such as the Riverside and Eagle Street Pier markets, which sell a diverse selection of products, from food to handicrafts.

▼ *Brisbane River*

▲ Bamboo Grove,
City Botanic Gardens

CITY BOTANIC GARDENS

At Gardens Point are the much-treasured, lush City Botanic Gardens. The mature gardens offer fabulous views of the Brisbane River and Kangaroo Point Cliffs, located opposite, and are a wonderful spot for walking, picnics or even catching an outdoor movie at certain times of the year. The gardens opened in 1855 but even before the gardens' official opening, the site was used from 1825 to grow food for the penal colony.

A CULTURAL HOTSPOT

South Bank, on the southern bank of the Brisbane River, is a popular leisure and cultural precinct. It comprises extensive parklands, called the South Bank Parklands, with numerous restaurants, cafes and bars and the quirky Streets Beach, a man-made beach. Some of the city's major cultural institutions, including the Queensland Performing Arts Centre, the Queensland Museum, the State Library of Queensland and QAGOMA – the Queensland Art Gallery and Gallery of Modern Art – are found at South Bank within the Cultural Centre. Fortitude Valley, also known as 'the Valley', is one of the city's upcoming, trendy areas and a shopping and entertainment destination.

Many significant cultural and sporting events have been held in Brisbane, including the 1982 Commonwealth Games, World Expo '88 and the Goodwill Games in 2001. The Brisbane Festival, which takes place every year, is a spectacular celebration of the arts.

▲ Formal Annual Garden,
City Botanic Gardens

▶ Queensland Performing
Arts Centre

QAGOMA

AN INNOVATIVE ARTS INSTITUTION

QAGOMA, the collective name given to the Queensland Art Gallery and the Gallery of Modern Art (GOMA), is the state's leading visual arts institution and a major Brisbane attraction. QAGOMA is known for its innovation in programming, especially for children and families. The two galleries sit just 150 metres apart in South Bank's Cultural Precinct. They display a broad variety of historical and contemporary works by Australian and international artists. More than 1 million people visit the Queensland Art Gallery and GOMA each year.

▲ *Young visitors creating in the Paramodel joint factory project during Kids' APT7*

GALLERIES, OLD AND NEW

The Queensland National Art Gallery has a long history, stretching back to its opening on 29 March 1895 in a room in the old Town Hall building. The original collection included just 38 pictures, a marble bust and 70 engravings. Today, the Queensland Art Gallery has a permanent home on the Brisbane River. The building, designed by Queensland architect Robin Gibson, opened on 21 June 1982. That year the gallery was awarded the Sir Zelman Cowen Award for its distinctive design. A new glass-encased entry, also designed by Robin Gibson, was added in 2006, coinciding with the launch of GOMA.

In July 2002, Sydney architectural firm Architectus was commissioned to design the Gallery of Modern Art at Kurilpa Point, next to the Queensland Art Gallery. GOMA opened on 2 December 2006. Its collection comprises artwork of the 20th and 21st centuries.

AN ART CENTRE JUST FOR KIDS

The Queensland Art Gallery has long recognised the importance of young people's appreciation of art. In 1941 a children's art class began. A selection of drawings produced in the classes was displayed in 1953 – the gallery's first exhibition of works by kids. In 1998 the gallery put on its first exhibition specifically aimed at children, called 'Portraits are People Pictures'. The following year the first-ever Kids' APT, part of the Asia Pacific Triennial of Contemporary Art series, was launched. Next the gallery began the Toddler Tuesdays program, allowing children as young as 18 months old to explore art. The Children's Art Centre, housed at GOMA, offers an engaging program of hands-on exhibitions and activities for children of all ages across both galleries. One of its biggest events to date has been the Kids Contemporary Australia Summer Festival in 2009, which drew more than 50,000 visitors.

▼ Left: *Yayoi Kusama's interactive children's project, 'The Obliteration Room', 2011.*
▼ Right: *Visitors created 6500 planes at Alfredo and Isabel Aquilizan's In-flight project during Kids' APT6*

Gold Coast

FUN IN THE SUN

The Gold Coast, situated 94 kilometres south of Brisbane, is the second largest city in Queensland, the sixth largest in Australia and one of the country's top holiday destinations. A key part of the city's appeal is that it has many attractions for a broad range of ages and interests.

The Gold Coast welcomes more than 4 million overnight visitors, mostly from within Australia. China, New Zealand and Japan account for the largest numbers of international tourists.

With a pleasant subtropical climate, the Gold Coast offers 70 kilometres of uninterrupted coastline featuring world-famous sandy beaches and excellent surf breaks, and thrilling theme parks. Some of the Gold Coast's most popular theme parks include Dreamworld, Sea World, Warner Brothers Movie World, Currumbin Wildlife Sanctuary and Wet 'n' Wild Water Park. In addition, the city is well known for its glamorous style, with high-rise buildings, extensive shopping areas, upmarket restaurants and a bustling nightlife.

▲ *Surf Carnival, Kirra Beach*

The Gold Coast is home to a range of high-profile events throughout the year, such as the Magic Millions racing carnival, the Iron Man Series, the Coolangatta Ocean Swim and the Quicksilver Pro and Roxy Pro surfing events. In 2018 the city will host the Commonwealth Games.

◄ *Surfers Paradise*

A SURFING PARADISE

At the heart of the Gold Coast is Surfers Paradise, the area's entertainment and tourism hotspot. Originally the town was called Elston. Following the opening of the Surfers Paradise Hotel in 1925, the town's name was changed to Surfers Paradise. The town's development accelerated through the 1950s when the first holiday apartments and shopping strips were built. Today its skyline is dominated by high rises.

SCHOOLIES

Each year in November and December thousands of Year 12 graduates flock to Surfers Paradise to celebrate the end of their school days. Called 'Schoolies', the event is the country's largest celebration of school-leavers.

HINTERLAND

In the nearby Gold Coast Hinterland is Lamington National Park, an area of superb subtropical rainforest, which is part of a World Heritage-listed area known as the Gondwana Rainforests of Australia.

▼ *View to Morans Falls from Python Rock Lookout*

Sunshine Coast

A TOURIST MECCA

Located north of Brisbane (but still within Southern Queensland), the Sunshine Coast is an area of long, beautiful beaches, rivers, lakes and subtropical forest – and a mecca for tourists – that stretches from Bribie Island in the south to Rainbow Beach in the north.

A number of favourite holiday destinations, such as Maroochydore and Caloundra, and major attractions, such as Australia Zoo, near Beerwah, and the UnderWater World marine park, in Mooloolaba, are found on the Sunshine Coast. Noosa Heads is the region's upmarket tourist destination, with numerous luxury hotels, restaurants, cafes and bars and high-end shopping.

▲ Caloundra Beach

GLASS HOUSE MOUNTAINS

In the region's south are the spectacular Glass House Mountains, a group of 11 craggy peaks that dominate the surrounding area. These are the eroded remains of volcanoes, known as volcanic plugs. Mount Beerwah, at 556 metres above sea level, is the highest of the peaks. For the traditional owners, the Gubbi Gubbi people, the area was a meeting site for ceremonies and trade and remains a place of great cultural importance today. The peaks, which reminded James Cook of glasshouses, were named by him during his voyage of 1770 along the east coast of Australia. The first European to explore the area was Matthew Flinders who climbed Mount Beerburrum in 1799. The peaks are protected within Glass House Mountain National Park, which is a popular place for picnics, bushwalking and climbing.

▲ Glass House Mountains

Fraser Island

K'GARI – 'A BEAUTIFUL PLACE'

Fraser Island, a World Heritage-listed site, extends 123 kilometres along Queensland's southern coast. At its widest point it is 25 kilometres across. The island, covering an area of 1840 square kilometres, is ranked as the largest sand island in the world. Fraser Island is the largest island in Queensland and the sixth largest island in Australia. The island was included on UNESCO's World Heritage List in 1992 for its outstanding natural universal attributes.

Protected within Great Sandy National Park, the island is a place of rare beauty with more than 250 kilometres of unspoiled sandy beaches, cliffs and sand formations in vivid colours, remarkable desert-like sand blows, ancient subtropical rainforest set on sand and pristine freshwater lakes and streams. Fraser Island is separated from the mainland by the Great Sandy Strait, which has been listed under the Ramsar Convention as a Wetland of International Importance. The traditional Aboriginal owners, the Butchulla people, call Fraser Island *K'gari* or *Gari*, meaning 'a beautiful place', which captures the essence of the island well.

SHAPESHIFTERS

The island has a complex system of coastal dunes that are constantly evolving. Fraser Island's dunes are of great geological value because they provide a record of climatic and sea level changes over 700,000 years. Its highest dunes are some 240 metres above sea level. The island features a range of fascinating dune formations, such as the sand blows, which are shifting masses of sand carried by strong winds. The sand blows sometimes cover vegetation, even smothering entire forests. There are approximately 43 blows on the island. Coloured sands, stained yellow, orange, red and brown by minerals, are found underneath some of the blows where the sand has bound with clay. When the sandmass is swept away, the coloured sands appear, and in some instances – such as the Pinnacles and Red Canyon – astounding sculptural formations emerge.

▲ *Coloured sands*

UNUSUAL PHENOMENA

One hundred freshwater lakes are found on the island; some are crystal clear, others are brown-coloured, caused by decomposing vegetation. The island has 40 perched dune lakes – half the number of known lakes of this kind in the world – including the largest perched lake (Lake Boomanjin) and some of the highest ones (Boomerang Lakes). Fraser Island's lakes are fringed by white-sand beaches and make ideal swimming spots. Lake McKenzie is a favourite spot among tourists.

Sand environments are not usually associated with areas of dense vegetation. However, on Fraser Island a wide variety of plant communities thrive, including rainforest, woodland, mangrove forest and coastal heath with beautiful annual wildflower displays. Fraser Island's towering rainforest communities, featuring trees as high as 50 metres, are a most unusual phenomenon. In fact, they are the only tall rainforests in the world that grow on sand dunes at elevations of more than 200 metres.

▲ *Lake McKenzie*

Fraser Island has relatively few mammal or aquatic species but is home to a variety of birds, reptiles and amphibians. Its bird population consists of more than 350 recorded species, particularly seabirds and shorebirds. The island is well known for its dingo population, which has had little exposure to domestic or feral dogs. Its dingoes are thought to be the purest strain in eastern Australia and perhaps even all of the country.

CONNECTIONS WITH COUNTRY

The Butchulla people have lived on the island and the adjacent mainland area for more than 5000 years. Extensive archaeological evidence of their occupation has been found on the island in the form of shell middens, artefacts, scarred trees (markings produced where bees' nests have been removed) and campsites. The arrival of European settlers severely affected the Butchulla people's way of life. By the end of the 19th century, most of the island's Aboriginal inhabitants were relocated to a reserve on Fraser Island and eventually to the mainland. The Butchulla people have maintained their spiritual and cultural connections with their country.

▲ *Wangoolba Creek*

Wet Tropics

WORLD HERITAGE ANCIENT RAINFOREST

The Wet Tropics region, which features World Heritage ancient tropical rainforest, runs along the eastern escarpment of the Great Dividing Range from Cooktown to Townsville. At 130 million years of age, it is the oldest continuously surviving area of rainforest on the planet. Covering approximately 8940 square kilometres, the Wet Tropics contains magnificent landscapes of mountains, rivers, waterfalls, beaches and, of course, lush rainforest. It has enormous ecological significance, with hundreds of rare and threatened plant and animal species. The Wet Tropics region was awarded World Heritage status in 1988.

A WINDOW INTO EVOLUTION

The plant life found in the Wet Tropics World Heritage Area represents a window into the evolution of plant life on the planet. Many of the plant species within the area can be traced back to when Australia was part of the supercontinent Gondwana. The region has tremendous diversity, with 13 major types of rainforest. It is also home to the greatest number of flowering plant families in the world found in one location.

▼ *Fan palm tree canopy, Daintree National Park*

IMPORTANT WILDLIFE

The fauna found in the region is highly valued. About a third of Australia's marsupial species live in the Wet Tropics, 58 per cent of its bat and butterfly species, 40 per cent of its bird species, 29 per cent of its frogs and 20 per cent of its reptiles. In total, more than 50 animal species are endemic – that is, they are found nowhere else. One of these is the musky rat kangaroo, the most primitive surviving kangaroo species.

WHERE THE FOREST MEETS THE SEA

Much of the Wet Tropics is protected as national parks, conservation reserves and other reserves. The most famous of these is the Daintree National Park, north of Cairns. It has two sections, the northern Cape Tribulation part and the southern Mossman Gorge part. Both Cape Tribulation and Mossman Gorge are well-known natural attractions.

Cape Tribulation is a stunning area where rainforest-covered mountains slope down to long unspoiled beaches. It is a famous landmark in Australian history. In 1770 British explorer Lieutenant James Cook's ship, HMB *Endeavour*, ran aground when it hit a reef that is part of the Great Barrier Reef. He named the headland 'Cape Tribulation' and the reef 'Endeavour Reef'. Jeannie Baker's award-winning picture book *Where the Forest Meets the Sea* was inspired by the Cape Tribulation area.

MOSSMAN GORGE

At the tranquil Mossman Gorge pristine water tumbles over granite boulders. The waterholes, which are surrounded by lush rainforest, are ideal for swimming. It is also a great place to discover the area's rich Aboriginal heritage. The traditional owners of this country are the Eastern Kuku Yalanji people. Visitors can join Dreamtime walks, guided by local Aboriginal people, to learn about their culture.

RAINFOREST PEOPLE

In addition to the Eastern Kuku Yalanji people, a number of Aboriginal groups have connections with the area that stretch back for at least 5000 years and as long as 50,000 years. These groups are thought to be the first Aboriginal occupants of Australia and the oldest rainforest people in the world.

▲ *Mossman Gorge*

▲ *Mossman River*

The Great Barrier Reef

A WORLD HERITAGE AREA

Covering a vast area of 348,000 square kilometres, the World Heritage-listed Great Barrier Reef is the largest coral reef system on Earth and an area of immense natural beauty. Stretching more than 2000 kilometres along Queensland's east coast from Cape York in the north to Bundaberg in the south, the reef consists of around 3000 separate coral reefs and 900 islands. The reef was inscribed on the World Heritage List in 1981 for its outstanding universal value. It was the first coral reef system to be named a World Heritage Site.

▲ *Aerial view of the Great Barrier Reef*

INCREDIBLE BIODIVERSITY

Built by billions of coral polyps, the reef is the world's largest structure made by living organisms. The Great Barrier Reef supports an incredible range of marine creatures, some of which are vulnerable or endangered. It has some of the greatest diversity of life on the planet, including approximately 1500 species of fish, 360 species of reef-building corals, 4000 species of molluscs and 1500 species of sponges. In addition to the coral reef ecosystems, it also consists of more than 2000 square kilometres of mangroves and 43,000 square kilometres of seagrass meadows. Other significant marine animals, such as the dugong, humpback whales and the endangered loggerhead turtle, come to the reef to feed, calve or nest, in the case of turtles. More than 200 bird species use the islands and coral cays.

▲ *Coral colony*

GREAT SCENIC VALUE

The Great Barrier Reef is one of Australia's most visited natural sites, with more than 1.6 million visitors each year. It is one of the world's most desirable locations for scuba diving and snorkelling. While many visitors choose to take daily boat tours from mainland cities, such as Cairns, there are many resorts on the reef's islands, those on the Whitsunday Islands being among the most popular. One of the iconic sites within the reef is known as Heart Reef, coral which has naturally taken the shape of a heart, located in the Whitsundays.

A PROTECTED MARINE AREA

The reef is protected within the Great Barrier Reef Marine Park, which allows tourism, fishing, boating and shipping in certain areas. It is managed by the Great Barrier Reef Marine Park Authority and is considered to be one of the world's best managed marine environments.

The Great Barrier Reef faces a number of environmental pressures, including from fishing, pollution, plagues of the coral-eating crown-of-thorns starfish and climate change, which leads to warmer ocean temperatures, resulting in coral bleaching. The crown-of-thorns starfish, which attacks coral polyps, occurs naturally in healthy reef environments, but in recent years poor water quality and reduced predators have allowed starfish numbers to increase.

A RICH CULTURAL HERITAGE

Aboriginal people and Torres Strait Islanders have lived in the area for many thousands of years. More than 70 groups have strong ongoing connections with their land and sea country. There are a number of archaeological sites within the Great Barrier Reef World Heritage Area, such as fish traps, middens and rock art, which reflect this long occupation.

CAIRNS

Cairns is the main centre in Queensland's Far North. It is the gateway to the Great Barrier Reef and the Wet Tropics. The traditional owners of Cairns are the Gimuy Walubara Yidinji people, who have lived in the area for many thousands of years.

Its European history dates back to 1770, when British explorer James Cook, aboard the Endeavour, mapped the area, naming the inlet on which Cairns is now based 'Trinity Bay'. The discovery of gold at Palmer River in 1872 drew prospectors to the area – they were the first non-Aboriginal inhabitants of the Far North. Cairns developed as a centre for the thriving agricultural industry around the settlement and on the Atherton Tableland, with the main products being sugar cane, fruit and dairy. It was officially declared a town in 1903.

▲ *Green turtle*

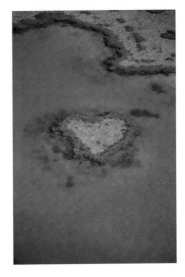

▲ *Heart Reef*

Cape York Peninsula and Cooktown

REMOTE BEAUTY

The Cape York Peninsula, in Far North Queensland, is one of Australia's most remote and beautiful places. The tip of Cape York is the most northerly point of mainland Australia. Known as one of the country's last frontiers, the peninsula is bordered by the Gulf of Carpentaria to the west and the Coral Sea to the east. The peninsula features vast areas of unspoiled native vegetation, including tropical savanna, wetlands and rainforests, and a stunning coastline characterised by white dunes and turquoise water.

▲ Tip of the Cape York Peninsula

A RICH CULTURAL HERITAGE

In addition to its great scenic value, the Cape York Peninsula has a rich cultural heritage. Most of the peninsula is the traditional country of more than 40 tribal groups with different languages and cultures. The peninsula has extensive splendid rock art galleries, particularly those at Quinkan, as old as 30,000 years.

▼ Engraving of the Endeavour River where the Endeavour was brought ashore for repairs, William Byrne, 1773

AUSTRALIA'S FIRST EUROPEAN SETTLEMENT

Cooktown, the administrative and cultural hub of the peninsula, has the distinction of being Australia's first European settlement – if only briefly. It was here, at the mouth of the Endeavour River, in 1770, that Lieutenant James Cook and the crew of HMB *Endeavour* set up camp for seven weeks to repair their ship's hull, which had been badly damaged on the Great Barrier Reef. During this time Cook and his crew met with the local Aboriginal people, the Guugu Yimithirr, on a number of occasions, which was documented in his journal. This has been described as the First Reconciliation between Europeans and Aboriginal people.

Cook and his crew members, including illustrator Sydney Parkinson and botanist Joseph Banks, recorded a list of about 150 Guugu Yimithirr words. This was the first written record of any Indigenous Australian language. Among the words documented was the name of the animal the local people called *gangurru*, transcribed as 'kanguru' – which of course became the English word kangaroo.

It was also here that Joseph Banks collected and preserved samples of around 200 specimens of plant life. Together with his journal entries, which included notes on the plants and animals he discovered, these provided a record of many new species for the Western world, such as acacia, banksia (which carries Banks's name) and eucalyptus.

A THRIVING PORT TOWN

Approximately 100 years later, during the late 1800s, Cooktown became a bustling port and community servicing the Palmer River goldfield. It was the second largest town in Queensland at the time.

COOKTOWN TODAY

Today the town's population is much smaller, consisting of about 2000 people. Each year, for more than 50 years now, a re-enactment of Cook's landing, which incorporates the perspective of the Guugu Yimithirr, is performed. The James Cook Museum, in the former St Mary's Convent, traces the history of Cooktown including Cook's seven-week stay. The collection includes the *Endeavour*'s anchor and cannon, which were recovered from the reef.

▲ *Rock art at Laura, Cape York*

▲ *Watercolour of* Banksia Serrata *by John Frederick Miller,* 1782

Torres Strait Islands

STEPPING STONES TO OUR NEIGHBOURS

At the tip of Cape York Peninsula are the Torres Strait Islands, a group of islands scattered between mainland Australia and Papua New Guinea. More than 247 islands are dotted over an area of 48,000 square kilometres, almost like stepping stones to our northern neighbour, Papua New Guinea. The northernmost island in the strait, Saibai Island, is just four kilometres from Papua New Guinea. Only 13 of them are inhabited. The islands belong to the state of Queensland. The main administrative and commercial centre of the region is on Thursday Island.

A FASCINATING CULTURAL HERITAGE

The Torres Strait Islands have a fascinating cultural heritage that dates back thousands of years to a time when there was a land bridge between Australia and Papua New Guinea. The Indigenous people of the region, known as Torres Strait Islanders, are Melanesian, like the people of Papua New Guinea. They are distinct from Australia's Aboriginal peoples. There are 18 island communities within the Torres Strait. Two islander communities are located on Cape York Peninsula, also known as the Northern Peninsula. The Torres Strait Islanders have maintained strong ties with their land and sea country.

▶ *Waier Island*

EARLY EUROPEAN EXPLORATION

In 1606 explorer Luís Vaez de Torres was the first European to navigate the waters between Australia and New Guinea, but did not lay claim that he had seen the Australian mainland. Torres Strait was later named in his honour. On 22 August 1770 Lieutenant James Cook landed on Possession Island and claimed sovereignty over the eastern part of Australia on behalf of King George III of England. A monument is found near the site where Cook took possession of Australia's east coast. Cook noted the presence of Indigenous people on the nearby islands, particularly the Kaurareg people of Prince of Wales Island, or *Muralag* – the largest of the islands in the Torres Strait. In 1879 the Torres Strait Islands were annexed to the state of Queensland.

▲ *Murulag man,*
Prince of Wales Island

A NATIVE TITLE REVOLUTION

The islands featured in a landmark legal case, which became known as the *Mabo* case. In 1982 a Torres Strait Islander from Murray Island, or *Mer*, called Eddie Koiki Mabo, together with four other Meriam people, began legal action to establish their traditional ownership of the land. They argued that they were entitled to the land as they had a continuous connection with Murray Island and the surrounding reefs.

After a ten-year battle in the Supreme Court of Queensland and the High Court, on 3 June 1992 the High Court found that the Meriam people were entitled to the full ownership, occupation and use of Murray Island. The decision rejected the idea that prior to European settlement, Australia was *terra nullius*, that is, a land belonging to no one. It was the first time native title was recognised in Australia. This opened up the possibility for other Torres Strait Islanders and Aboriginal groups to claim rights to their traditional land. In response to the historic *Mabo* decision, the following year the Native Title Act 1993, which provided a legal framework for native title claims, was passed. Sadly, Eddie Mabo died just five months before the High Court's decision was handed down. Eddie Mabo is now a household name in Australia.

The Gold Coast attracts more than 10 million visitors each year.

Road rules apply on Seventy-Five Mile Beach, a sandy informal highway, which runs 120 kilometres along most of Fraser Island's east coast.

The Torres Strait Islands are the only part of Australia that shares a border with another country.

AT DAINTREE NATIONAL PARK TWO WORLD HERITAGE AREAS – THE WET TROPICS AND GREAT BARRIER REEF – MEET. IT IS THE ONLY EXAMPLE OF TWO ADJOINING WORLD HERITAGE AREAS IN THE ENTIRE WORLD.

PaulMorton; p. 120 Cape Leeuwin Lighthouse © iStock.com/FiledIMAGE; p. 121 Busselton Jetty © iStock.com/taolmor; p. 122 Giant tingle trees © iStock.com/isaxar; p. 123 The Pinnacles Desert © iStock.com/mddphoto; p. 124 Stromatolites © dr322/Shutterstock.com; p. 125 Cape Inscription Lighthouse, State Library of Western Australia BA558/225; p. 126 Whale shark © iStock.com/cdelacy; p. 127 Green turtle © attem/Shutterstock.com; p. 127 Cape Range © iStock.com/Jouke; p. 128 Cultured pearls, NAA: A6135, K1/2/74/7; p. 129 Dinosaur footprints © Kat Clay/Shutterstock.com; p. 130 Geikie Gorge © Janelle Lugge/Shutterstock.com; p. 131 Wolfe Creek Crater © David PETIT/Shutterstock.com; p. 131 Cathedral Gorge © Simon Krzic/Shutterstock.com; p. 132 Purnululu National Park © iStock.com/GCHaggisImages; p. 133 Mitchell Falls © Janelle Lugge/Shutterstock.com; p. 134 The Indiana Tea House © Adrian Lindley/Shutterstock.com; p. 134 Perth skyline © Robyn Mackenzie/Shutterstock.com; p. 134 The Pinnacles Desert © iStock.com/mddphoto; p. 135 Stromatolites © dr322/Shutterstock.com; p. 135 Whale shark © iStock.com/cdelacy; p. 135 Fremantle Harbour, NAA: A6180, 23/10/73/44; p. 135 Wolfe Creek Crater © David PETIT/Shutterstock.com; p. 135 Cathedral Gorge © Simon Krzic/Shutterstock.com

NORTHERN TERRITORY

p. 137 Map © Geoscience Australia; p. 138 Darwin skyline © iStock.com/JohnCarnemolla; p. 138 Wood engraving by Samuel Calvert, National Library of Australia, vn2833899; p. 139 Darwin Post office ruins, AWM 044607; p. 140 Crocodile © iStock.com/koshar; p. 140 Mindil Beach © iStock.com/Ladiras; p. 141 Great white egret © Piotr Gatlik/Shutterstock.com; Water lilies © Ivonne Wierink/Shutterstock.com; p. 142 Aboriginal rock art, Kakadu National Park

© Sean Lema/Shutterstock.com; p. 142 Jim Jim Falls © Janelle Lugge/Shutterstock.com; p. 143 Nitmiluk Gorge/Ellenor Argyropoulos © Tourism Australia; p. 144 Nitmiluk Gorge © iStock.com/sigurcamp; p. 145 Devils Marbles/Nick Rains © Tourism Australia; p. 146 Alice Springs oasis © ANUJAK JAIMOOK/Shutterstock.com; p. 147 Henley-on-Todd Regatta/Steve Strike © Tourism Australia; p. 147 Portrait of Albert Namatjira, National Library of Australia, vn1192304; p. 148 Kings Canyon/Chris McLennan © Tourism Australia; p. 148 Kings Canyon © iStock.com/Ladiras; p. 149 Uluru/Masaru Kitano snaK Productions © Tourism Australia; p. 150 Kata Tjuta/Frontier Photo Safaris © Tourism Australia; p. 151 Uluru-Kata Tjuta National Park Handover/Leaseback Ceremony, 1985, National Library of Australia, an24341097; p. 152 Darwin skyline © iStock.com/JohnCarnemolla; p. 152 Mindil Beach © iStock.com/Ladiras; p. 152 Great white egret © Piotr Gatlik/Shutterstock.com; p. 152 Alice Springs oasis © ANUJAK JAIMOOK/Shutterstock.com; p. 153 Jim Jim Falls © Janelle Lugge/Shutterstock.com; p. 153 Nitmiluk Gorge © iStock.com/sigurcamp; p. 153 Devils Marbles/Nick Rains © Tourism Australia; p. 153 Darwin Post office ruins, AWM 044607; p. 153 Kata Tjuta/Frontier Photo Safaris © Tourism Australia

QUEENSLAND

p. 155 Map © Geoscience Australia; p. 156 Brisbane skyline © iStock.com/holgs; p. 157 Brisbane River © Flickr/Brisbane City Council; p. 158 Bamboo Grove © Flickr/Brisbane City Council; p. 158 City Botanic Gardens © Flickr/Brisbane City Council; p. 158 Image of Queensland Performing Arts Centre courtesy of Dylan Evans and QPAC; p. 159 *Paramodel* project © Mark Sherwood/QAGOMA; p. 160 Yayoi Kusama's project © Mark Sherwood/QAGOMA; p. 160 *In-flight* project

© Ray Fulton/QAGOMA; p. 161 Surf carnival/Lincoln Fowler © Tourism Australia; p. 161 Surfers Paradise © iStock.com/jennybonner; p. 162 Python Rock Lookout © Ashley Whitworth/Shutterstock.com; p. 163 Caloundra Beach © Martin Valigursky/Shutterstock.com; p. 163 Glass House Mountains © Denelzen/Shutterstock.com; p. 164 Coloured sands © col/Shutterstock.com; p. 165 Lake McKenzie © iStock.com/Ladiras; p. 165 Wangoolba Creek © Janelle Lugge/Shutterstock.com; p. 166 Fan palm tree canopy © Silken Photography/Shutterstock.com; p. 167 Mossman Gorge © Ralph Loesche/Shutterstock.com; p. 167 Mossman River © Ralph Loesche/Shutterstock.com; p. 168 Aerial view of the Great Barrier Reef © Martin Maun/Shutterstock.com; p. 168 Coral colony © Pete Niesen/Shutterstock.com; p. 169 Green turtle © iStock.com/MyViewPhotography; p. 169 Heart Reef © Mornee Sherry/Shutterstock.com; p. 170 Cape York Peninsula/Oliver Strewe © Tourism Australia; p. 170 Engraving by William Byrne, National Library of Australia, an9184938; p. 171 Cape York rock art/Margaret Tuckson © Tourism Australia; p. 171 *Banksia Serrata* by John Frederick Miller © The Trustees of the Natural History Museum, London; p. 172 Waier Island/Oliver Strewe © Tourism Australia; p. 173 Murulag man, Prince of Wales Island © Douglas Stewart Fine Books; p. 174 Surfers Paradise © iStock.com/jennybonner; p. 174 Green turtle © iStock.com/MyViewPhotography; p. 174 Sand dunes, Fraser Island/Peter Lik © Tourism Australia; p. 174 Waier Island/Oliver Strewe © Tourism Australia; p. 174 Fan palm tree canopy © Silken Photography/Shutterstock.com; p. 175 Python Rock Lookout © Ashley Whitworth/Shutterstock.com; p. 175 *Paramodel* project © Mark Sherwood/QAGOMA; p. 175 Aerial view of the Great Barrier Reef © Martin Maun/Shutterstock.com